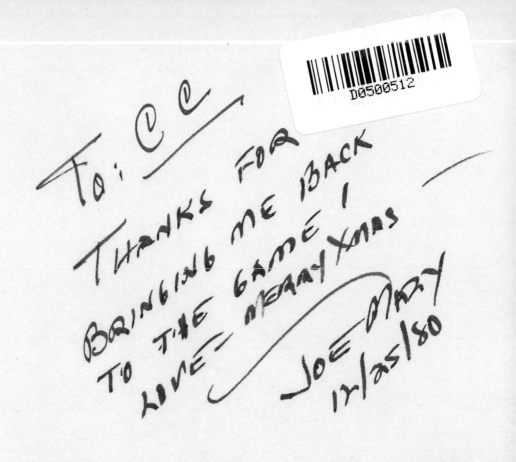

To: CC

THANKS FOR
BRINGING ME BACK
TO THE GAME !
LOVE — MERRY XMAS

JOE—MARY
12/25/80

THE NEW GOLF MIND

By Dr. GARY WIREN, PGA Professional
and Dr. RICHARD COOP, Educational Psychologist
with Larry Sheehan

ACKNOWLEDGMENTS

The authors wish to thank Hale
Irwin, Jim Jamieson, Davis Love,
Paul Runyan, Jim Simons and
Tom Watson for graciously
taking the time to read and
comment on the manuscript.

Published by
Golf Digest, Inc.
A New York Times Company
495 Westport Avenue
Norwalk, Connecticut 06856

Trade book distribution by
Simon and Schuster
A Division of
Gulf & Western Corporation
New York, New York 10020

First printing
ISBN: 0-914178-14-8
Library of Congress: 77-92911
Manufactured in the
United States of America

TABLE OF CONTENTS

PART I

GOLF AND THE TWO-SIDED BRAIN

1 MENTAL MIS-HITS

"I kept coming off the ball today."
"I was blocking everything out."
"I wasn't turning into the ball."
"I lost my tempo."
"I had no pivot."
"I couldn't keep my head down."
"I came up short on all my putts."
"I hit everything thin."
"I was dipping my right shoulder."
"I bent my left arm."
"I was casting from the top."
"I couldn't get off my right side."

When golfers make bad shots, they find mechanical reasons like these to account for what went wrong. But, in fact, in a large percentage of cases, mental—not mechanical—reasons may be the root cause of the mis-hits. For the majority of golfers it is the brain, not the body, that is causing most of the errors and costing so many strokes.

Take a moment to think about your own game.

Haven't you produced "pure" shots with each of the clubs in your bag at one time or another?

If you have split some fairway with a 240-yard drive at least once, doesn't it suggest that you may already have the mechanical skill to hit the driver correctly more often?

If you've hit good shots with all your irons, granted in a random fashion, doesn't it mean you must have the physical resources to produce good iron shots more consistently?

If you've escaped from sand once with the proper technique, doesn't it mean you can do it on a regular basis?

Have you ever smoothed in a putt from five feet? From 10 feet? From 15, 20, 25, 30 feet?

If you've made all these putts of varying lengths once or twice, doesn't it show you have a putting stroke that can be effective more of the time?

Do you have a ringer score for the course you

usually play—that is, a record of your best-ever score on every hole?

High-handicap golfers who have trouble breaking 100 on any given day nevertheless boast ringer scores in the 70's—because over the seasons they've managed to shoot par at least once on almost every hole on the course. Medium-handicap golfers have ringer scores in the 60's. Scratch players and pros have record scores in the 50's or even lower.

If golfers can "out-perform" themselves over the long haul in this manner, doesn't it suggest that they possess the physical ability, strength and coordination to "out-perform" themselves more often and on a more regular basis?

We think the answer is yes, and that it is the golfer's *mind* that is keeping the golfer's body from performing anywhere near peak efficiency, causing him to mis-think and mis-feel his way into high scores and low spirits out on the course.

The purpose of this book is to show how the mind—"the new golf mind" of our title—really does work and to provide the tools that will allow you, the individual golfer, to use your mind to best advantage in your own game.

2 THE TWO-SIDED BRAIN

The first thing to understand is the brain itself. In simple terms, there are two sides to every mind—literally two hemispheres of "gray matter" in the one brain—and each side has its own way of thinking and its own special functions.

A complex motor skill like golf requires the participation of both sides. In fact, we think golf may be unique among sports in the degree of participation *and* cooperation it demands of each hemisphere.

Many people may already be aware of the fact that, physically, the left hemisphere of the brain controls the right side of the body and that the right hemisphere controls the body's left side. Thus, a man who suffers a stroke in the left side of his brain risks paralysis in the *right* side of his body. This crossover effect is a mechanical aspect of the nervous system and not our main concern here. Rather, our interest lies in the special *mental* faculties that each side of the brain has developed.

The two hemispheres, which for convenience we shall label the ANALYZER and the INTEGRATOR, acquired their preferences for performing certain mental tasks in the course of human evolution.

The result is that with the ANALYZER, or left hemisphere, we now do most of our rational, critical, step-by-step thinking. The ANALYZER helps us verbalize, deduce, compute, solve problems logically. Speaking, reading, writing, ordering—all these activities are controlled primarily through the ANALYZER.

The INTEGRATOR or right hemisphere has become our specialist in creative and artistic endeavors and the instrument that keeps us in touch with our feelings and emotions. The INTEGRATOR has intuitive rather than analytical powers. It can help us make sudden insights and to visualize and create images. Also, and of great im-

THE TWO-SIDED BRAIN: GENERAL FUNCTIONS

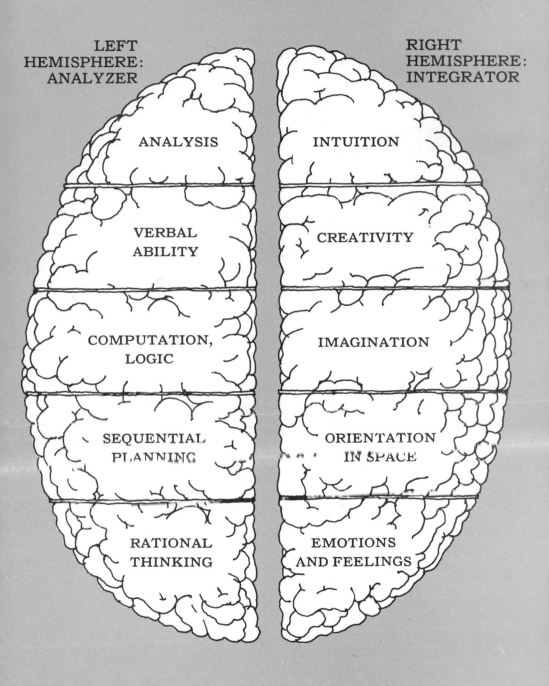

LEFT
HEMISPHERE:
ANALYZER

RIGHT
HEMISPHERE:
INTEGRATOR

ANALYSIS

INTUITION

VERBAL
ABILITY

CREATIVITY

COMPUTATION,
LOGIC

IMAGINATION

SEQUENTIAL
PLANNING

ORIENTATION
IN SPACE

RATIONAL
THINKING

EMOTIONS
AND FEELINGS

portance to motor skill performance, the INTE-GRATOR helps us keep our bodies oriented in space, in the proper relation to our surroundings.

(The five to ten percent of the population who are left-handed, incidentally, do not automatically follow this pattern of left brain being ANALYZER and right brain being INTEGRATOR. For many lefties, the pattern is reversed. But the challenge of understanding and functioning effectively with a brain consisting of two specialized hemispheres is exactly the same.)

You may ask—how do we know all this? In fact, though the two-hemisphere concept of how the mind works is a relatively new development, it already has a firm foundation in medical science and in neurological and physiological research.

Rehabilitation programs and testing involving victims of cerebral damage from accidents or strokes, for instance, have confirmed the existence of the specialization in functions mentioned above. A person loses some mental faculties when he suffers damage in one hemisphere, but other faculties remain stable.

Brainwave experiments have been conducted using electrodes and needles as stimulants to different areas of the brain, and these, too, have shown how different mental activities correlate to different sides of the brain.

The evidence of a "two-brain brain" is so extensive now, in fact, that major new educational and cultural philosophies have appeared on the scene, and many more may be expected. Lately even sex researchers have gotten into the act—with studies that proclaim that passion is exclusively a joy of the right hemisphere.

The point we're trying to make is that the two-hemisphere brain theory is not a figment of our own right hemisphere. It is an exciting and valid new concept with far-reaching implications—and with intriguing possibilities for golf. We'll use the two-hemisphere idea of the brain as a model for understanding the new golf mind throughout this book.

10

3 WHY YOU NEED BOTH SIDES OF THE BRAIN TO PLAY YOUR BEST GOLF

The drawing shows the special golfing faculties of the ANALYZER (left hemisphere) and the INTEGRATOR (right hemisphere) portions of your brain.

These resources, characteristic of each hemisphere, cannot be drawn on so easily as hot and cold water from a tap. But they can be identified, nurtured and mobilized for the purpose of better golf. Sometimes simply your awareness of how ANALYZER and INTEGRATOR function or interrelate can help your game.

The ANALYZER serves as evaluator and decision-maker during a round of golf. It assesses course and weather conditions and devises shot-making tactics for each hole. It checks the ball's lie and selects the club to be used for each shot.

Suppose, for example, you are facing a possible wood shot to a par-5 hole that must carry a creek just in front of the green to get home. Here's how your ANALYZER might function in solving this particular club-selection problem:

"Let's see, I'm downwind (as you throw some grass in the air) but the green is shallow, running mostly from left to right, and it's fairly flat and hard. There are bunkers in the back—and I'm not playing well out of this powdery sand today. I could get this shot home but with the flyer lie in this light rough it would never hold the green. If I don't hit it well, I could end up in the drink. So take a 5-iron—make that a 6-iron just to be safe—that still leaves me with a wedge for the next shot."

The ANALYZER may also be active in this situation in relation to *grip* ("I'll choke down and keep the shot low" or "I'll grip more firmly so the rough doesn't turn the club in my hand"), to *aim* ("Trouble on the left, play to the right half of the green"), and to *setup* ("Weight left, hit down on this shot to get it up quickly").

During a round of golf, the INTEGRATOR

serves as synthesizer and executor. It translates the relevant analytical information about each shot into a non-verbal, non-critical language of its own, which permits the body to execute the swing unimpaired by conscious thought or detail. Using its powers of imagination, intuition and feel, the INTEGRATOR visualizes shot patterns, senses body position and provides the estimation of effort required for those in-between swings on short shots.

Suppose, for example, you are confronted with a downhill pitch shot over a bunker. Your INTEGRATOR may help you visualize the shot by "seeing" the ball landing three feet short of the putting surface, taking two short bounces and trickling slowly down toward the cup. Then, in practicing the swing required to produce this shot, it tells you which rehearsal stroke has the length of backswing and degree of firmness appropriate to the shot. And, finally—provided you stay in the right hemisphere with that correct feeling—it allows you to reproduce with confidence the stroke for the actual shot.

Generally, many pre-shot activities are analytical in nature, so the conscious faculties of your brain can and should be active. But once the mind has gathered and processed the necessary pre-shot information and the body is ready to make the swing, the conscious faculties have to be put on stand-by status while the intuitive faculties help execute the shot smoothly. Mastering this switch from left to right brain—"giving up voluntary control at the perfect moment," as Michael Murphy says it in *Golf in the Kingdom*—is of the greatest importance.

A lot of golfers play the game almost exclusively with one hemisphere or the other, which is the mental equivalent of playing with half a set of clubs.

Knowing that the pin placement is back, for example, that the ball is wet and so won't spin as much, and that you are lined up properly in relation to the target, may be excellent work on the part of

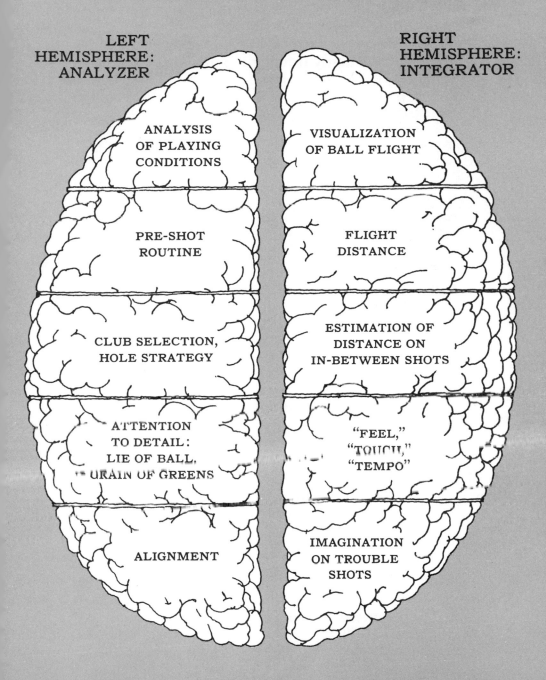

THE TWO-SIDED BRAIN: GOLF FUNCTIONS

LEFT
HEMISPHERE:
ANALYZER

RIGHT
HEMISPHERE:
INTEGRATOR

ANALYSIS
OF PLAYING
CONDITIONS

VISUALIZATION
OF BALL FLIGHT

PRE-SHOT
ROUTINE

FLIGHT
DISTANCE

CLUB SELECTION,
HOLE STRATEGY

ESTIMATION OF
DISTANCE ON
IN-BETWEEN SHOTS

ATTENTION
TO DETAIL:
LIE OF BALL,
GRAIN OF GREENS

"FEEL,"
"TOUCH,"
"TEMPO"

ALIGNMENT

IMAGINATION
ON TROUBLE
SHOTS

your ANALYZER, but such cognitive data will do you little good if you can't pull the trigger and swing freely after setting up to the ball.

Conversely, being able to make your best swing, particularly under pressure, may be a sign that your INTEGRATOR isn't afraid to do its thing. But if you have chosen the wrong club or gripped the club incorrectly or failed to allow for a strong crosswind, making your best stroke still won't produce the desired result.

These examples illustrate potential problem areas for all golfers. Sam Snead conceivably would have won many more tournaments if he had used his ANALYZER side more. By his own admission he seldom bothered stepping off yardages at tournament sites. And Ben Hogan might have won fewer, if he had used his ANALYZER less.

For most mortals before good golf can happen, there has to be a solid partnership of the two brain hemispheres, one which permits analytical modes and intuitive modes of thinking to play equal and complementary roles.

Many golfers, not understanding this division of abilities and responsibilities, frequently go to one hemisphere for something that only the other hemisphere can supply and botch shots that way. They analyze when they should be integrating, and they integrate when they should be analyzing.

Putting is the simplest example of an area of golf where each hemisphere plays a distinctly different, but equally important, role. Suppose you have a 30-footer. You must evaluate the green with your ANALYZER to figure out the line your putt will travel. Is there grain? Has the green been mowed today? Is the surface wet? Is there a slope to consider? With your INTEGRATOR, you must convert the information to feel for speed and direction.

Both hemispheres must be used to make the putt—or at least to give it your best effort. A diligent land surveyor may spot the correct line to his cup, but without feel or touch, he'll have another putt or two to finish the hole. The fellow with a safecracker's touch for distance will miss left or right just as often, if he chooses to ignore the type and texture of grass on the putting surface or its slope and contours.

We all probably know golfing friends who fit these descriptions—who, in effect, are using only half their faculties on the greens.

Can you remember the first time you were faced with a less-than-full shot to a green? You had learned how to make your full swing on the practice tee, but when it came time to hit that 9-iron or wedge 40 or 50 yards to the green, you probably couldn't do it. Chances are you put your full swing on it and airmailed the green. There was nothing wrong with your swing. It just didn't correlate to the shot required at the time. You made the same mistake as the diligent land surveyor in the previous example: you didn't use your INTEGRATOR to "sense" the distance you needed to cover, then reduce your swing, without spoiling your swing action.

Let's say you're in a 36-hole weekend tournament. In the first round, you par a certain 140-yarder, using a 7-iron off the tee to knock the ball 15 feet from the pin. Second day, same hole, you hit the same good 7-iron, but this time it lands short of the green, backs up and rolls down a bank into the water. You take a double-bogey.

What went wrong? On the second day, your ANALYZER failed to take into account that the tee markers were back 10 yards, that there was a 15 m.p.h. wind in your face and that the temperature was 7 degrees cooler. In short, your rational faculty should have informed you to hit a 5-iron, not the 7. The pros call a shot like this a "no-brainer." Actually, it's a "no-left-brainer."

Suppose your tee shot on a par 3 gives you the choice of hitting for the flagstick on the left over the corner of a pond or playing for the right-center of the green. The shot to the pin requires one longer club. If it is short, it will probably kick off the bank into the water. If it's long, it will go down a steep bank leaving a very tough pitch. The shot hit for the right center of the green, but landing short, will not catch the water. If it's long, it will roll into the collar grass or light rough. What to do? Certainly, in this case, your ANALYZER should recognize the wisdom of not shooting for the flag.

We are presenting these examples primarily to show you the broad differences in functions of the two hemispheres, but diverse as they are, it is important to realize that the hemispheres must work in tandem, as well as independently. Many mis-hit shots result when ANALYZER and INTEGRATOR are interfering with each other or are simply incommunicado.

We all have experienced split-brain interference in ordinary life. For instance, if you get very excited during an argument, you may notice you have trouble speaking clearly or thinking of the correct words to use. The right-brain emotions are blocking the left-brain verbal skills. Professional typists run into the opposite problem if they start trying to comprehend the material they are copying. Their word-per-minute rate goes down while their errors increase, because the left-brain analytical process is blocking the right-brain performing ability.

A recent research project clearly documents interference between hemispheres. The experiment had individuals balance objects on a finger of each hand simultaneously, first in silence, then while speaking. When the people were asked to talk at the same time, it was found they could not balance the objects held in the right hand for as long a period as the left hand. Without conversation, the left hemisphere managed the right hand's mechanical task fine, but when verbalization—also a task of the left hemisphere—was introduced, the job became more difficult.

A classic example of a golfer getting caught *between* hemispheres came during the final round of the 1977 Masters. Jack Nicklaus was preparing to hit a 6-iron to the 18th green, on which the pin was cut in the front. In need of a par to stay even with co-leader Tom Watson, Nicklaus visualized playing safely away from the bunker in front of the green, finishing within two-putt range with an outside chance at a birdie.

As he stood up to the ball to make the shot, a roar came from the huge gallery surrounding the 17th green—signifying Watson had birdied.

Nicklaus now realized he needed a birdie himself to get into any playoff and that the shot he had envisioned would not give him a realistic chance at it. He knew he had to hit a less-than-full 6-iron in order to finish nearer the pin.

Nicklaus knew what he needed to do with his ANALYZER, but he didn't give himself time to get used to the new shot requirement—to visualize the shorter approach with his INTEGRATOR. Result: he hit an extremely un-Nicklaus-type shot. He quit on the ball with his left side, his left wrist collapsed at impact, and he knocked it—and his chances— short and left into the bunker.

4 YOUR PSYCHOLOGICAL SCORECARD

An effective and enjoyable way to go about examining where and how your own ANALYZER and INTEGRATOR may be misfiring or out of sync is to construct a psychological scorecard for your round next time you play.

Take an actual scorecard and mark the holes where in your opinion you made a mental, emotional or psychological error. On what holes did either poor judgment or lack of judgment cost you strokes? Where did fear or anger hinder your stroke? Did you suffer from inattention or lack of concentration that produced shots of less than your best effort? Did your left hemisphere "talk to you" and cause internal distractions during the playing of any shots?

Make your assessment as soon after the round as possible—while everything is still fresh in your mind. Also, get at least one of your more congenial playing partners to join you in doing it. Another player's perspective may add a dimension to your behavior that you hadn't considered or even reveal something you hadn't noticed at all. You, in turn, can learn interesting points about the problems other golfers have and also about how a round of golf in itself tends to pose psychological challenges at certain points more than at others (see illustration pages 24-25).

Once you've isolated the mistakes, analyze them in terms of the two-hemisphere model.

Here, for example, are 10 different "mental errors" from among many reported to us by scores of players, ranging in ability and experience, along with our interpretation of what really caused the mis-hit or cost the stroke.

> "I was just short of the green on one hole and had an easy chip to the pin, but instead of Texas-wedging it with my putter or one of the

straighter-faced clubs, I decided to lob it up to the hole with my pitching wedge, because I figured that's the way a pro would do it. I had no feel for the shot and hit it over the green."

This is a simple case of bad judgment. The ANALYZER was mis-informed: most pros would have putted the ball from the fringe. The INTEGRATOR may have sensed it was the wrong situation for a wedge, but with the wrong club in hand, there was nothing much it could do about it.

"I had pulled out a 3-iron for my approach on a hole, but when I got over the ball I was sure I had too much club. Instead of going back to my bag, I decided to swing easy and finesse it, but I quit on the shot instead, hit it thin and left the ball 20 yards short of the green."

In this case, the ANALYZER realized it had made a mistake in its initial club selection but the golfer was too lazy, embarrassed or indifferent to do anything about it. It relied on the INTEGRATOR to make up for its failing, which was beyond the INTEGRATOR's ability to do so.

"On a short par 5, I was getting ready to hit my second shot, a 3-wood that I thought would finish just short of the green. I'd visualized the shot clearly. Then the fellow I was playing with took his shot from farther away and to my surprise he reached the green. Now, as I stepped up to my ball, I thought I might be able to reach the green, too. But I didn't give myself enough time to get used to the new mental picture. I swung too hard and topped it 40 yards."

This is a case of a golfer trapped between hemispheres—similar to the Jack Nicklaus shot in the Masters we described. The golfer wasn't in his old plan when he went up to the ball, but he hadn't incorporated his new plan, either. The ANALYZER was confused and hadn't made contact with the INTEGRATOR yet.

> "I had to hit from a sandy lie in some light rough on the left side of the fairway. I approached the shot carefully and felt I did everything I needed to do. I played the ball back a little in my stance, got my weight on the left side and had the clubface slightly closed. Then as I took the club back, I said to myself, 'But you don't want to overdo it!' I shanked it into a trap on the other side of the fairway."

An impressively well-informed ANALYZER knew how to cope with the trouble shot, but then wouldn't let his partner, the INTEGRATOR, perform. It butted in with words where it had no business, after the swing had started.

> "I snap-hooked my drive into the woods on the hole where the prize for the longest drive was a dozen balls."

The "longest-drive" flag stuck in the fairway commonly brings out the "macho" element in men's events. If the ANALYZER had been on its toes, it would not have read the flag as distance, but rather danger—the danger of overswinging. It failed to register so the INTEGRATOR went hog wild.

> "I had a 30-foot putt and as I was lining it up, my partner said, 'Whatever you do, don't leave it short.' So I knocked it about 20 feet past."

This variation on the normally sensible "never up—never in" piece of putting advice did not work here because the golfer's INTEGRATOR was not permitted to perform its role of gauging distance intuitively on short shots. The fact that the putt went so far beyond the cup clearly shows that the ANALYZER was in charge and was determined to make the putt long, not short.

> "I missed an 18-inch putt and on my way to the next tee all I could think about was how I had blown it for my partner. Then when it was my turn to tee off, I hit it O.B."

Out-of-bounds because of inattention. The golfer's ANALYZER was still on the preceding shot and on what it had cost the "team," so it could not properly prepare or stimulate the INTEGRATOR to make the good swing.

> "I'd been driving well all day, but we came to a hole where there was water on the left side and woods on the right. My opponent hit first and hooked the ball into the water. I got up and did the same thing."

Into the water because of the INTEGRATOR's unique ability to mimic swings—bad swings as well as good ones. A sharper ANALYZER in this instance might have been able to prevent this fairly common occurrence by focusing on a specific mechanical factor in the setup or swing for its own tee shot, thus blocking the bad picture that the INTEGRATOR had just been exposed to on the opponent's shot.

> "We were even coming onto the 18th tee. There I pointed out to my opponent, who was new to the course,

that there was an out-of-bounds on the right side. I guess I hoped to scare him a little. He hit his tee shot straight down the middle, though. Then it was my turn to hit and all I could think of was that O.B. I tried to hook it left but I sliced it right."

Out-of-bounds because of *reverse* copying. The gamesmanship backfired because the golfer's ANALYZER created an idea that was supposed to influence the opponent. Instead, his own INTE-GRATOR picked up on it. Then, in going out of his way to avoid what he felt so keenly, he tensed up and sliced instead of hooked.

"My opponent hit a 5-iron over the green on a par 3, and I wondered if maybe the ball he was using, a Topflite, was 'hot.' I was playing a Titleist, but I had some Topflites in my bag and I thought maybe I should hit a Topflite with a 6-iron instead of a Titleist with the 5-iron. I stuck with the Titleist, but eased up on the 5-iron and finished way short of the green."

Hair-splitting by the ANALYZER resulted in indecision, preventing the INTEGRATOR from making the normal 5-iron swing which probably would have put the ball—any brand of ball—on the green. An esoteric or minute concern such as this is fairly common among better players, but when left unresolved, it can disrupt the right-brain machinery.

5 SAVING SHOTS WITH YOUR PSYCHOLOGICAL SCORECARD

There are two reasons why the psychological scorecard is a valuable tool for golfers, not merely an exercise in Monday-morning quarterbacking.

First, it creates an awareness about individual shot execution that allows the golfer to process bad shots without getting upset about them or tinkering with swing mechanics unnecessarily.

Take the golfer who had snap-hooked his tee shot on the "longest-drive" hole. If this golfer failed to perceive the outside factor that caused him to change his normal swing—to hit all out instead of swinging within himself—he might have decided there was something awry in his technique. "I'm hooking the ball," his ANALYZER might have decided on the next tee, "so I think I'll open my stance more"—with one possible consequence being that he *slices* the next one.

Or take the golfer who had putted the 30-footer 50 feet. If he failed to understand that he had left his INTEGRATOR out of his routine for that one putt, he might have become embarrassed at his dismal performance, or infuriated, or so concerned over the big miss that it might shake his confidence in his putting for the rest of the round.

The second reason scorecarding the mind game is useful is that it builds awareness of *general* traits in our psychology which alone may be sufficient to help us improve.

For example, the first time the three authors of this book played golf together, it was supposed to be just for fun. We had been talking all day about the various non-mechanical aspects of golf, and we merely wanted to relax for nine holes before grabbing a quick dinner and returning to work.

We did relax and enjoy the break. But immediately afterwards, we decided to construct a psychological scorecard for our own rounds.

Sure enough, we discovered that we, too, had

TOM	5	5	3	7	4	5	4	3	4	40
HOLE	1	2	3	4	5	6	7	8	9	OUT
BLUE	400	415	340	490	184	485	416	166	404	3300
MEN'S PAR	4	4	4	5	3	5	4	3	4	36
	DIDN'T WARM UP - NOT READY	NEGATIVE THOUGHT ON IRON SHOT - THINKING - HOOK	GOOD MENTAL IMAGE	D.R. RIGHT. WIND LEFT TO RIGHT MADE ME TIGHT - BLOCKED	TOO MUCH CLUB. DIDN'T ALLOW FOR WIND	PULLED MY PUTT - AFRAID WOULD MISS IT RIGHT	FIGHTING - HOOK THOUGHTS	ANOTHER PUSHED IRON -	PULLED IRON HERE - OVERREACTED TO LAST IRON SHOTS	
									BETTER IRON SHOT	

DATE   SCORER

HOLE	1	2	3	4	5	6	7	8	9	OUT
BLUE	400	415	340	490	184	485	416	166	404	3300
MEN'S PAR	4	4	4	5	3	5	4	3	4	36
TOM	5	5	3	7	4	5	4	3	4	40
DRIVE	1	1	/	(⁰	↑	1	1	\	)	
2ND SHOT	\	λ	1	\		1	⊤	⊤s	/	
3RD SHOT	/	⊤		⊤ ⊤s			\	⊤		
PUTTS	/ 2	\ 2	7 1	/ 2	↑/ 3	\ 2 5	1 15 1	/ 2		

Top card shows how a golfer might jot down mental or mechanical miscues during a round or immediately after.

Bottom card shows a highly detailed profile of the same round exclusively in terms of mechanics. Golfers need not keep track of every aspect of play, as is done here, to benefit from such an appraisal. This comprehensive charting system describes strokes with these symbols:

	11	12	13	14	15	16	17	18	IN	OUT	TOTAL
4	4	6	4	5	4	5	4	5	41	40	81
0	11	12	13	14	15	16	17	18	IN	OUT	TOTAL
75	200	470	330	495	350	355	180	500	3255	3300	6555
4	3	4	4	5	4	4	3	5	36	36	72
O.K.	WIND AGAIN - THIS TIME SHORT - GOT TO THINK BETTER	TRIED TO HIT IT TOO HARD - FROZE	INTO GRAIN ON PUTT - LEFT IT SHORT	PUSHING - PUTTS OR LEAVING SHORT - TOO TIGHT	PITCH SHOT SHORT - ALLOWING FOR TOO MUCH RUN	NOT ENOUGH CLUB - TRIED TO HIT HARD + HIT FAT INTO WATER	DIDN'T COMPLETE ROUTINE ON 2ND PUTT - TRY	PUTT STILL TO RIGHT			

ATTEST

10	11	12	13	14	15	16	17	18	IN	OUT	TOTAL
375	200	470	330	495	350	355	180	500	3255	3300	6555
4	3	4	4	5	4	4	3	5	36	36	72
4	4	6	4	5	4	5	4	5	41	40	81
↘	T	⌐°	/	|	|	|	/	↘			
|	↑	|	|	/	↖	T w		T			
		/	|	\	T	/		/			
T 2	T 2	/ 2	T 2	/ 2	10 1	20 1	↗ T 3	/ 2			

Symbol	Meaning
|	straight shot
\	pull
/	push
)	hook
(	slice
T	short
↑	long
s	sand
w	water
o	out-of-bounds

Putts are charted with the same symbols. The first putt is described in the upper left-hand corner of the "putts" box. Total number of putts are recorded in the lower right-hand corner. On one-putt holes, distance in feet is given in the lower left-hand corner.

Thus, on the second hole, Tom bogeyed by 1) driving straight, 2) pushing his second shot short, 3) just missing the green in three, and taking two putts for a 5.

thoroughly misplayed what Louise Suggs once called the hardest golf course in the world—the six-inch layout between our ears.

In nine holes, it appeared that among the three of us we had managed to throw away a total of 15 shots not, strictly speaking, because of mechanical errors, but because of mental lapses which led to mechanical errors.

The professional golfer on this writing team threw away two strokes, he figured. The good amateur player—a 7-handicapper—lost four strokes. And the 20-handicap golfer blew about nine strokes.

Double these figures to arrive at a cost in strokes over a full 18-hole round and you can see why it might have been hard for the pro to shoot par on this particular day. It would have been harder still for the good amateur to break 80. And it would have been almost impossible for the high-handicapper to break 95 or even 100.

The point is, one simple, relatively painless postmortem allowed all three of us to discover ways to improve our own games without becoming hung up on technical swing faults.

The 20-handicapper, for example, learned not to rush his pre-shot routine when playing with superior golfers, and the next time he played in like company he managed to finish the round without scoring over 6 on a single hole—the first time he had ever achieved such consistency.

The 7-handicapper discovered that his swing portrait of himself as a left-sided "puller" had been erroneous; in fact, he was a right-sided "thrower" and all the mechanical things he had been trying in order to draw the ball and add more distance to his drives had been self-defeating. With a more accurate self-concept, he was able to understand the root of his problem, make some simple adjustments and add an average of 10-15 yards to his tee shots.

The pro realized that he tended to get caught "between hemispheres" on shots when playing in a group that lacked another pro or someone else who could offer real competition. If he changed his mind about club selection, for example, he was inclined to stay with the wrong club because nothing was really riding on his shotmaking.

Afterwards, he saw the danger in playing in a "de-aroused" state without being aware of it. He thought his confidence could be affected by thoughtless club selection or mis-hits, or that he might be tempted to alter his technique without good reason.

With this new awareness, the pro felt better equipped mentally to play in similar situations in the future. He decided he would arouse himself for the occasion via some outside means, such as setting a scoring goal for the day, or he would play that round strictly for fun, not letting the shots he played with less than normal attention affect him, no matter what their outcome.

6 ANALYZER GOLF

In this hang-loose, Eastern-philosophy-influenced age of ours, it is not particularly fashionable to promote the values of the analytical left hemisphere. But that is what we must do here, because golf provides some very special challenges that could not be met without the help of the ANALYZER.

Consider how much easier it is to play out of sand if you use your left hemisphere properly.

If you understand that the ball escapes the bunker from the force of the concussion of the sand and not directly from the impact of the face of the club, as is true on all other shots, then it is much easier for you to accept and implement the technique of hitting behind the ball—and subsequently make the effort to acquire the specially flanged sand wedge suited to the job.

Once you know that the concussion force is a key in the sand shot, you are also in a position to logically determine variations in the technique for different situations. Since very light, fluffy sand compresses easily, it's important to hit farther behind the ball. But the ball comes out of wet sand faster, because wet sand is already compacted, so you don't have to take as much sand when you swing.

Consider uneven lies. If the ball is above your feet, you'll tend to hook; if it's below your feet, you'll tend to slice.

If your ANALYZER takes the time to understand that principle, you won't have to depend on rote memory to adjust your aim properly in compensating for the natural drift of a shot out of such lies. That is, if you realize that the reason for the hook is that the clubface of any lofted club simply points more to the left of the target line when the club is elevated because of terrain, then you'll never become confused when you face such a shot. You'll be able to check it out logically during your pre-shot routine and aim a bit right of your target to offset the hook.

How about club selection? Why do you think tour players know when to tee off with a driver and when to retreat to a 2-iron?

Because they have accumulated solid left-hemisphere knowledge about their driving patterns. Let's assume a pro knows he can land a tee shot in a 40-yard-wide fairway 80 percent of the time, but that for one 30 yards wide, his rate of success drops to 60 percent. When the pro faces the narrower version and finds it is bordered by water on the right and sand on the left, his ANALYZER will look at the percentages and inform him to select the 2-iron.

This book is not about *learning* golf, but about playing it more effectively. Yet, we would be remiss not to mention why the ANALYZER's rational perspective on things is essential in taking up the game in the first place. It helps us face up to the realities of golf and to overcome the built-in obstacles to mastering the game. No one can "flower" spontaneously into becoming a good golfer.

There are three things in particular that would drive most people crazy with frustration if they did not have their left-hemisphere thinking cap on in trying to acquire the fundamentals of the game. They are:
  —the contradictory nature of golf technique;
  —the lack of positive transfer from other sports in trying to learn it; and
  —the delay in getting satisfaction while mastering the sport.

Golf's seeming contradictions stem from its being a highly unorthodox motor skill. Kids with their natural mimicking ability may be able to pick up the game quickly in a caddieyard, ignoring the contradictions, but adults have to work at it.

Compare the golf grip with the grip in tennis: A tennis professional tells his new pupil to "shake hands" with the tennis racquet and moments later the pupil has a start on a fine forehand grip.

There's no way a golf professional can get a new student to spontaneously assume anything closely resembling a correct grip for golf.

It is a cliché to say that the golf swing is a study in opposites, but it is true. In baseball to hit to left field, you swing in the direction of left field. In golf, you can swing left and have the ball slice to the right. If you swing to the right, the ball can hook left. You have to hit down on the ball to make it go up. If you try to lift it up, you'll top it. If you swing hard—at almost 100 percent effort—your muscles tighten and the ball lands short. If you swing with less strength, say 85 percent effort, it goes farther.

Your INTEGRATOR doesn't fathom why maximum effort won't produce maximum distance and so will favor an all-out attack on the ball. But your ANALYZER reads and accepts findings that show the clubhead actually slows down with maximum effort. That realization paves the way for swinging within yourself, thus ensuring your best distance on your drives.

We don't have to understand the physics involved when our car goes into a skid on an icy highway to know what to do. All we have to remember, in the interest of our fenders, is to turn the car in the direction of the skid. In other words, even if your ANALYZER is not an MIT graduate, it has to overrule your INTEGRATOR, whose instinct to turn the car in the opposite direction of the skid would only increase the skid.

Similarly, we don't have to fully understand the mechanical principles that explain all the apparent contradictions in learning golf, so long as our ANALYZER sees there are sound reasons and motivates us to acquire the fundamentals in a straightforward manner from a good instructor.

By *positive transfer* we mean using skills acquired in one activity to help you along in another activity. A lot of learning occurs this way. You can pick up squash quickly if you've already played tennis, because both sports are similar.

But golf has many components which differ

from those found in other sports. Natural athletes with great records in other sports turn to golf and have to start from scratch. Frequently, they get negative transfer instead of positive transfer from the sports in which they've excelled. If they try to get through just on their right-hemisphere instincts, they fail. That's why home-run king Hank Aaron once quipped, "It took me 17 years to get 3,000 hits in baseball. I did it in one afternoon on the golf course."

On the other hand, many people with ordinary physical talents rise to respectable heights in golf. They accept the laws of the game, do what their pros tell them to do and practice long hours to build a sound grip, stance and a consistent swing action. All in the great left-hemisphere, nose-to-the-grindstone tradition. And it works.

The *delay in gratification* from the game makes many people quit golf before they find out what it's all about. And it can seriously impede learning in those who stay with the game, but lack the patience to sharpen their grasp on the fundamentals.

There are fast learners, to be sure. One young woman we know went from novice to 6-handicapper in three summers. The first year she was not allowed to play, only to swing and hit on the practice tee. The second year she was taken out on the course and in her first round she shot 87. The third year she was scoring in the 70's and became club champ. The first 72-hole tournament Larry Nelson ever played was on the PGA tour. Only two seasons earlier he had been a 12-handicapper; now he's considered a budding young star on the PGA circuit.

These two people obviously had a lot of natural talent to start with, but they also benefited from outstanding instruction and a carefully planned program that, in effect, protected them from early disappointments and frustrations. Both also devoted more hours to learning the game than most beginners probably could give.

But it's tough to develop consistency in golf. It takes many players a year or more to develop enough skill and confidence to step out on a golf course with any reasonable hope of satisfaction. Those who do go out sooner (and most of us do) compound playing problems with learning problems.

The lesson here is that if we don't use our ANALYZER to justify the hard-work/low-pay conditions we face in learning golf, then we may become discouraged and disenchanted with the game.

We must call on the ANALYZER later on, too, in rebuilding a faulty swing or coping with some other persistent new problem in our game. Arnold Palmer early on tediously rebuilt his swing, and it took him months to get through the ordeal. He shot in the 80's instead of the 70's for one long summer as he gradually brought the improvement under control. This change eventually allowed him to produce rounds in the 60's, and that's when his star began to rise.

7 INTEGRATOR GOLF

We may learn the key positions of the golf swing with the ANALYZER's help, but we execute the swing primarily with the INTEGRATOR.

The right hemisphere's special body-in-space intuitive powers are what allow us to integrate the elements of the swing into one fluid, continuous motion. Musical ability is carried in the right hemisphere, and we believe the *tempo* of a good golf swing originates from this side of the brain as well.

Integration and tempo. Meshing of the gears. Putting the pieces together. One swing, one fluid motion, not forward press— takeaway— backswing— downswing— follow-through, etc.

In ballrooms or in discotheques, you can readily distinguish the natural dancer from the person who learned by dance-step diagrams in the mail.

Similarly, on a golf course, you can always spot the pupil who has acquired all the correct swing positions, via his ANALYZER, but who has not yet allowed the INTEGRATOR to put them together for him.

Without help from the INTEGRATOR, our swings are likely to be overly mechanical, powerless, inconsistent and even incompatible with our true physical and psychological make-ups. More important, the swings will collapse more easily under stress.

Consider that point in the swing when the backswing ends and the downswing begins. This is a moment in time that all golfers must master subjectively, so they can make the transition away from the ball back toward the ball with ease and consistency.

An attempt to pinpoint the transition via the ANALYZER might go as follows:

At the end of the backswing, the left heel is raised slightly off the ground. The left knee is flexed, pointing to the ball. Weight is felt on the inside of the right foot. The left arm is extended with hands stretched skyward, the straight left wrist matching the clubface plane. Club points on a line parallel to the target line. The downswing begins as the left heel returns to the ground. Knees thrust toward the target, shoulders start to unwind and the arms start to swing down.

Here's an attempt to pinpoint the transition via the INTEGRATOR. It is the description Bill Mehlhorn, a great and colorful tour player of the 1930's, used to give his pupils:

"Flip a penny in the air and watch it rise, then fall. Did you see any sudden change in direction? No. Now that's the way a golf swing progresses from backswing to downswing. It just happens."

The highly detailed view of what occurs may be correct in every particular, but there is no way the golfer can absorb all the data in the middle of the swing. It won't help him make the transition smoothly. Indeed, it would hinder, confuse, paralyze.

The simpler view may offer an analogy that your INTEGRATOR can pick up on and respond to. It cues the body to go through all the steps perceived as necessary by your ANALYZER without consciously doing so. "Let your muscles do your thinking," is how Sam Snead describes this phase of the action.

The point is, an overloaded left hemisphere can do nothing to help you start the club down correctly. A properly cued right hemisphere can handle the job with remarkable finesse.

We once observed a low-handicap amateur, in-experienced in instructing, literally destroy a good golf swing in a matter of minutes through overly technical, though well-intentioned, advice.

First, his pupil made a nice rhythmic swing, but topped the ball.

"Don't lift your head up," said the teacher.

His pupil made another fairly good swing, but this time he had less motion in his lower body. In concentrating on keeping his head down, he also kept his weight back. He hit behind the ball this time.

"Don't stay on your right foot on the down-swing!" said the teacher.

Now the pupil went through his setup at a noticeably slower pace. His next swing was tighter and his left arm was bent. He sliced it.

"You can't bend your left arm like that!" cried the teacher.

The pupil's fourth swing—which was the last one we could bear to watch—was now totally devoid of rhythm. He whiffed the ball.

Teaching professionals with a heavy lesson schedule often remark on the difficulty of playing well themselves. That's why Wee Bobby Cruick-shank used to refuse to give a lesson for 30 days prior to any important tournament he intended to play in. The little Scot felt he needed more than a wee amount of time to clear his left hemisphere of analytical teaching ideas.

Former touring star Chick Harbert notes, "A lot of people know how to swing a golf club, but they've gotten so involved in swing mechanics that they've lost track of the main goal, which is to come in with a low number."

Harbert's own teaching method involves "purg-ing" the golfer's mind of all that complicated think-ing, and it's been successful. One pupil came to him as a 59-year-old, 14-handicap player and wound up winning his club championship three seasons later.

"The funny thing is that the man's fellow members can't figure out what he is doing differently," says Harbert. "Well, he's just *thinking* differently, and that's something they can't see."

Many golfers, teachers and pupils alike, don't give the INTEGRATOR a chance to help the golf swing because they don't trust it. Our Western society happens to be organized around the ANALYZER's view of things. Creativity in our children falls off sharply after second grade because the kids are going full speed learning multiplication tables, diagramming sentences and doing various other analytical tasks of the left hemisphere. Our government, our way of doing business and our legal system are monuments to the ANALYZER's thinking style. As products of this culture, we tend to operate out of the left hemisphere whether or not we work in government, business or law. And our golf games may suffer for it.

These cultural conditions have been changing, of course. In the past decade, various right-hemisphere philosophies have made inroads into our lives. Today corporate executives are almost as likely to be into Transcendental Meditation ("TM"), yoga or the *I Ching* as are poets and artists. Professional athletes and sports instructors are not just reading *Psychocybernetics* and *The Power of Positive Thinking*—products, par excellence, of our Western culture. They are also checking out *The Inner Game of Tennis* and *Zen and the Art of Archery*—viewpoints on self-management which are derived in large part from Eastern cultures. Even the skeptics among us have discovered that a number of the ideas and techniques "imported" from outside our traditional civilization can help people function better in their personal and professional lives.

We're saying you need both. You can't just skip merrily into playing flawless "inner golf" with your right hemisphere. But you must begin to plug into that side of your brain regularly after assimilating the fundamentals of the game.

PART II

TOOLS OF THE NEW GOLF MIND

Building the bridge between thought and action

A bundle of closely wound nerve fibers called the *corpus callosum* connects the two hemispheres of the brain. A kind of communications network, the *corpus callosum* serves as a bridge between the specialized faculties and functions of the two hemispheres, as shown in the illustration, right.

This bridge can be used or abused in golf. If ANALYZER and INTEGRATOR are sending conflicting messages to each other, for instance, the resulting traffic jam on the "bridge" would lead to a poor swing or a mis-hit. If ANALYZER and INTEGRATOR are sending *no* messages to each other, the shot that results probably would be "indifferently played," as Henry Longhurst used to say. Once we were in a foursome with a fellow whose mind was a million miles away. On one hole, we pulled the flag for him to putt and went over by the edge of the green, whereupon he putted directly toward the flagstick we were holding. Now that's indifference.

In any case, the trick in golf is for you to use the *corpus callosum* to help produce a good swing consistently. *Verbal, visual* or *kinesthetic* messages sent across the bridge can be effective in achieving this.

BRIDGING THE GAP BETWEEN
THE TWO HEMISPHERES
WITH SWING CUES

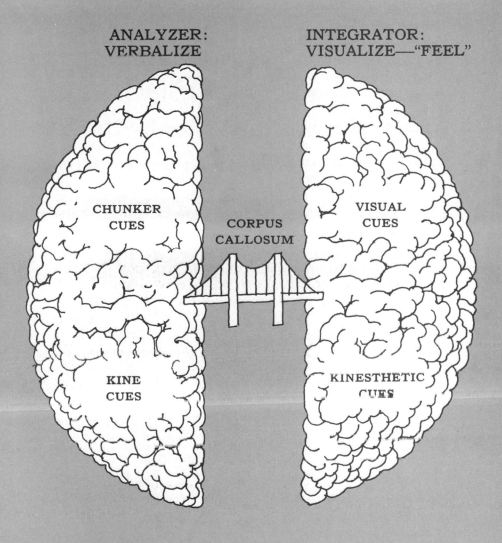

ANALYZER:
VERBALIZE

INTEGRATOR:
VISUALIZE—"FEEL"

CHUNKER
CUES

VISUAL
CUES

CORPUS
CALLOSUM

KINE
CUES

KINESTHETIC
CUES

8 VERBAL SWING CUES

Recently, one of the authors taught archery at summer camp. For the opening class, he dutifully prepared six pages of closely typed mimeographed material, then handed it out and began going over it page by page. After 20 minutes of this, a red-headed kid in the front row reached up, tugged on his shirt and said pleadingly,

"Hey, when we gonna shoot?"

Clearly, an overly verbal approach to learning can be boring—especially for kids. But it would be foolish for adults to discount the power of words to communicate just because we are living in an age of TV and picture magazines. In fact, words or phrases that are simple, memorable, golf-appropriate and relevant to the golfer's individual style can be a great help in building and maintaining a solid golf game.

Locating verbal swing cues that are effective and that suit your own style is basically a left-hemisphere activity. The ANALYZER must search, find and distill the essence of the swing into a word or phrase to which the INTEGRATOR can respond.

The reason so much care has to be taken by the ANALYZER in picking the word or phrase has to do with how things stick in a person's memory. Tests have shown that words play the major role in this process.

For example, two separate groups of people were given this picture to look at:

Those who were told to remember it as a ship's wheel reproduced the picture a week later as:

Those who were told to remember it as the sun reproduced it as:

The word rather than the actual image used to remember the picture had more influence on the way it was stored in memory.

That's why in golf it's important to couch all cues in positive, golf-appropriate language.

Suppose, in the course of a round, an extra-long tee shot is required. If the words you use to summon this effort out of yourself are, "Hit it hard!" chances are you'll produce a poorly struck or extra-wild drive. That's because the abrupt, staccato words you've chosen encourage tension and almost beg for the smaller muscles in your hands and arms to contract.

But if you say, "Free-wheeling through the ball" or "light arms 'n full turn," you'll more likely nurture the use of the longer body muscles, and thus create a more fluid swing action.

There are two somewhat different types of verbal swing cues: kinematopoetic, or what we'll call kine cues, and chunker cues.

Kinematopoetic or kine cues

Every student in high school English class is taught about the onomatopoetic device in poetry. If a poet describes equestrian traffic with the words, "clippety-clop, clippety-clop," the phrase is onomatopoetic because it actually sounds like horses' hooves on the pavement. So is bees buzz or rain going splish-splash.

Something kin-e-mat-o-po-et-ic (kine, pronounced kin-ee, refers to body movement) would be a word or phrase that reflects the image or recaptures the stored feeling of a particular movement like a good golf swing. For easy usage, let's call it a kine cue. It helps elicit in the golfer the response of the appropriate swinging action.

Sam Snead has a one-word kine cue—"oily"—to remind himself of how he likes his swing to feel. It does not so much describe the golf swing itself as it connotes the overall *feeling* of the swing action. That is why, while the selection process by which such cues are chosen depends on the ANALYZER, the key to their success depends on provoking some golf-appropriate response in the INTEGRATOR.

Betty Hicks used to carry around a driver that had written on it: "Ooooom . . . . . . PAH!"—an utterance that captured the rhythmical relationship of backswing to downswing for her and helped her cue a whole set of muscles to interact properly and deliver maximum force through the hitting zone.

Other golfers have devised tempo cues like, "Well, hello. . . . Dolly!" or the circus ringmaster's resounding, "Ladies and gentlemen!" to trigger proper backswing-downswing rhythm.

Rhythm cues are not easy to communicate on paper. Try them out by swinging your arms back and through as though you were holding a club, at the same time reciting the cue.

The cues can apply to any particular type of swing called for on the course. In fact, all trouble shots require more powerful imaging, because they are less familiar than the run-of-the mill shots (if there are such things in golf) and also because they normally put more pressure on the golfer.

One golfer's kine cue for hitting out of dry sand is: "Splash!" For hitting out of wet sand: "Splat!" A super putter we know said his secret on the greens was feathers. "Whenever I go to putt," he said, "I think of the word 'feathers.' " The word "feathers" is kinematopoetic for him because it evokes a nice light touch in his stroke.

Chunker cues

Chunker cues are more "rational" than kine cues in the sense that they generally convey a fairly accurate description of one or several aspects of the swing. While kine cues can use nonsense words (so long as they influence the right hemisphere properly), chunker cues generally stick to solid analytical words.

The concept of chunking originated in a psychological study that showed most people could handle no more than seven separate pieces of information at the same time without their left hemisphere blowing a fuse. The phone company made use of this study when, expanding their system, they had to issue new and longer telephone numbers. By teaching people to learn their phone numbers in chunks or sets, few people resisted the change.

For example, the number at PGA headquarters in Florida would be hard to remember presented as

3058483481

but chunk them using parentheses and a hyphen

(305) 848-3481

and it's a cinch. Now the number consists of only three units of information.

Chunking allows you to "dial" your swing, the way you can dial phone numbers familiar to you, without thinking about the component parts. The really good teachers in golf provide this service for their pupils all the time. They take several "bits" of information and "chunk" them into one word, phrase or sentence.

Noted instructor Bill Strausbaugh chunks the short game into three words: "triangle, track, target." When his pupils step up to hit a short shot, they set arms and shoulders in a triangular configuration, then simply swing their triangle along the track to the target.

But the most important distinguishing feature about chunker cues is that they pinpoint an integral action in the swing which, if successfully executed, automatically causes several other vital things to happen. In this respect, the chunker cue is quite different from the usual golf tip like, "Keep your left arm straight" which affects only one part of the swing—arc width.

Harry Pressler says to his pupils, "Put your right elbow in your pocket on the downswing." Result: the pupil (1) leads into the swing with the left side; (2) swings with good timing; (3) swings down the target line; and (4) swings with the proper angle of attack.

"Elbows together at the top, elbows together at the finish," says Harvey Penick. The student hearing this cue (1) sets the club in the proper position at the top, (2) makes a true swinging motion and (3) avoids casting from the top or blocking out.

One of Bobby Jones' favorite instructional thoughts was, "Hit past your chin." If you try it, it may (1) keep you centered, (2) discourage an early hit, (3) increase square contact and (4) assist in your timing.

The titles of many golf instruction books actually refer to chunker swing cues that the various authors have discovered: *One Move to Better Golf, The Magic Move in Golf, Secret to the Golf Swing, Swing Easy—Hit Hard, Swing the Clubhead, Master Key to Success at Golf.* These and others are selling an action in the golf swing that, when performed correctly, causes a half-dozen other things to happen correctly in the swing.

Instructional material can be useful if it doesn't overwhelm the golfer and handicap his cuing ability.

A club pro we know once attended a week-long seminar on teaching golf, culminating in an informal tournament for all the pros who were there. By the end of the week, the pro had so many ideas about the golf swing that he did not think he knew how to start a backswing without giving it a name and number. His ANALYZER was hopelessly confused. So on the eve of the tournament, he skipped the banquet and went out on the golf course by himself. He played three balls for about nine holes, slowly but surely divesting himself of the excess knowledge he had gained and finally arriving at one chunker cue to help him draw the club back on the next day. "Turn back—turn through," he thought and won the event.

The best time to establish swing cues of any kind is when you're playing well. What does your swing feel like to you at those times, and what verbal tag can you put on it? The more accurately you pin down the feeling of the swing, the easier it will be to retrieve it at a later date and so to repeat the same good performance. It's not enough to experience a general appreciation for your good swing, when you've got it. Let the ANALYZER in on what the INTEGRATOR is feeling and create a swing cue out of it. Then write it down. These feelings are tenuous and elusive at best. If you don't make a note of them as they come to you, you're likely to forget them.

None of the swing cues mentioned here may work for you, not only because words evoke different strokes in different folks, but because the cues must connect with your individual style.

For example, if you're a Palmer-style hitter, as opposed to a Snead-style swinger, you probably have to hold onto your club more firmly. So Sam Snead's cue to grip lightly, as though "holding a bird," would be inappropriate—your club would do the flying if you tried it.

9 VISUAL SWING CUES

Visualization is one of the most potentially useful faculties of the intuitive, right-hemisphere INTEGRATOR. There have been numerous examples in many activities of its value in learning and in changing behavior and even in dramatic medical case histories.

This mind's eye of ours has three main applications for golf:

— seeing the desired line of flight for a shot;
— imaging the swing;
— mimicking favorable elements in the swings of other players.

"Seeing" the line

Seeing the line of flight for a shot is a kind of mental skywriting and many pros and teachers have commented on it. Indeed, the informed gallery-goer has heard the expression used so often that, standing by the ropes at a tournament, he himself may sometimes picture all the visualizations, with the result that the air space above the nearby fairway suddenly fills up for him with thousands of gracefully curving dotted lines.

Two things make it easier to visualize the path of your shot:

(1) *Experience*—The more often you have seen a 9-iron shot float down from high in the air, bounce twice and come to a stop 10 feet from the pin, the more readily you will be able to conjure up that particular flight pattern. Beginners can't see a flight trajectory in their mind's eye because they haven't seen it enough with their naked eye.

(2) *Confidence*—When you're playing well, you tend to see the line of flight you want to see. But when you're playing poorly, you can't see any lines, or the lines go to the wrong places.

One way to foster your INTEGRATOR's natural bent for seeing is to take the time to absorb the sight of a good shot when it happens. Don't try to *analyze* the trajectory in terms of height at apex, degree of curve and such, but stay with it with your naked eye so that a sense of the overall shot pattern becomes more ingrained in your right hemisphere.

The more you collect these impressions of good shots in play or on the practice tee, the easier it will be to conjure them up in your mind's eye when you face situations that require similar shots.

Needless to say, the flight patterns you imagine must conform to your shotmaking ability. There's a difference between wishful thinking and realistic visualization. If you fade most of the time, don't expect to "see" a hook drive, just because you're teeing off on a dogleg-left hole that seems to beg for a right-to-left shot.

The imaginary patterns also should offer reasonably safe passage among the hazards present. If you visualize a line of flight that takes your ball within 10 yards of an out-of-bounds, that in itself could make you nervous enough to mis-hit.

Golfers sometimes make a hard shot out of a routine approach by insisting on going for a pin tucked in the corner behind a bunker, instead of playing for the center of the green. They miss the shot not just because it may go beyond their ability to pull it off, but because of the unnecessary mental tension they create in picturing what they think is the pro shot to play.

In all of these situations just mentioned, visualization powers are actually used *against* the golfer, not *for* him. It is up to the ANALYZER to prevent this by controlling the choice of imagery just as, in developing verbal swing cues, it controls the choice of words.

On the greens, for example, you may find it better to visualize a track for a putt that is the width of the hole, rather than a razor-thin line to the middle of the cup. The picture of the wide track may keep you more relaxed and prevent flinching or tightening up.

"Imaging" the swing

There are swing cues which consist of words but owe their effectiveness primarily to the fact that they trigger more vivid swing *images.*

"The swing is a wheel, and the golfer is the hub." That is probably one of the oldest visual swing cues we have, and the fact that it is still around testifies to its applicability as a swing image and also its simplicity, which puts it within reach of a lot of golfers.

Other familiar cues of this genre are:

"Coil and uncoil."

"Turn in a barrel."

"Pivot around a fixed center."

"Feel the clubhead as though it were a stone on the end of a rope."

But we are not limited to the tried-and-true in visual swing cues any more than we are limited to clichés in verbal swing cues.

In fact, if the cues have no life or vitality to them, chances are they won't mean a thing to your INTEGRATOR no matter how often you try to invoke them.

Conduct the search for your own visual swing cues when you're playing your best. What does the swing "look like" to your intuitive faculty at these times? That's how you're most likely to find a workable visual cue of your own.

When he has to play a trouble shot, Jim Simons first pictures everything happening in his swing in slow-motion. This visualization helps him execute the shot with precision and at his normal tempo.

We have a friend who claims his favorite visual cue—that of a giant sheet of plywood representing his swing plane (reminiscent of the famous sheet-of-glass illustration of Ben Hogan's swing in *The Modern Fundamentals of Golf*)—not only gets him lined up correctly on every shot, but aids him in swinging in plane every time. As he approaches from directly behind his ball, he images the plywood sheet at the proper tilt on the line of flight. Then he steps "into" an opening in the plywood and sets his club behind the ball. Now he's ready to start the club back on the plane created by the plywood and return down and through on a similar plane.

Good visual swing cues put the golfer "in the picture," and sometimes more than that.

A psychologist by the name of Richard Suinn has worked with Olympic skiers with great success in this area, and it has definite application to golf. He calls this more elaborate form of visualization "body-thinking" because, when it works, the body seems to be as involved as the mind in the practice session.

Working indoors, Suinn once wired his racers to an electromyograph—a machine that picks up muscle activity—then asked them to imagine skiing down a particular course. For those skiers most successful at body-thinking, the machine recorded muscular bursts that matched perfectly with the more difficult passages in the race course. As the racers visualized going down the mountain, they also literally felt themselves exert different kinds and degrees of muscular effort.

In another interesting case involving sports, two groups of basketball players were recruited out of a school's physical education program and enlisted in an experiment to compare the potential benefits of different methods of improving shooting skills.

One group devoted 15 minutes a day to actually practicing free throws out on the court. The other group spent the same time sitting in the locker room—merely visualizing making free throws. At the end of the experiment both groups were given a proficiency test in free throws. The first group, it was found, had improved more, but the group that had practiced only mentally had also improved and almost as much. The statistical difference in rates of improvement was insignificant.

The conclusion clearly was that visualization or mental practice can often aid performance as much as physical practice.

The ability to visualize and to have a keen imagination in golf is especially important in the short game. The full swing doesn't require as precise judgment for distance—that's been taken care of in the club selection process. Direction is more the problem. On three-quarter shots, however, and practically any shot within 100 yards of the green, distance becomes a matter of feel. How far back should you take the club? How forcefully should you strike the ball? How much height should you get on the ball?

Your INTEGRATOR is invaluable in these situations if you use it to physically pre-feel, or mentally rehearse, the swing that is going to be necessary to do the job. But your ANALYZER has to recognize this capability in its partner, then trust it to do it.

As with "seeing" the line, experience and confidence make feeling the swing easier. But there is no question that they are within the ability of every golfer, and that they can be extremely effective in aiding any motor skill performance.

Mimicking

The legendary mimicking ability of young people is purely a function of the brain's intuitive faculty. The older we get and the more highly developed our ANALYZER becomes, the more resistant we are to using our INTEGRATOR's inborn knack of imitation. Yet, it can have an extraordinary effect on our golf games.

One day a club pro hurried directly from a tour of a golf club factory to the first tee at a course where he was scheduled to play in a local pro-am. With barely time to change into his spikes, he nevertheless produced for his opening tee shot one of the longest and straightest drives of his career, one that traveled well over 300 yards.

How did it happen? The pro realized later that his mind had temporarily absorbed the Bionic Swing during the last phase of his tour of the golf club factory—when he had watched a mechanical club-testing machine flawlessly strike about 100 balls in succession. The picture of this swing was so pure in his mind that he momentarily became the machine a bit later on the first tee.

The point is at times the right hemisphere can easily pick up information about the golf swing that the left hemisphere can get only at great cost. Touring pros welcome the chance to be paired with Snead or Boros or Weiskopf, not to learn any trade secrets, but to have these players' great tempos rub off on them a bit. The most popular golfers on college teams are not the scramblers but the excellent strikers of the ball. They're the ones their teammates want to practice with—they know instinctively their own swings can improve that way.

Club golfers can take advantage of their innate mimicking ability in the same way. For example, if you lose your timing you can try to regain it by playing with someone with a good swing rhythm or joining the gallery at a pro tour event for a round and allowing your INTEGRATOR to absorb the tempo of players who are on their game. Watch the good swing in its totality, not in all its bits and pieces.

This action-by-osmosis effect can backfire since, at the club level, bad swings outnumber good swings. If you let your INTEGRATOR indiscriminately tune in on other swings, it could cause a problem. Some golfers refuse to watch a left-hander hit a ball—the southpaw swing confuses them. Overexposure to the extra-quick windshield-wiper swing, or the swing of the fellow who literally jumps at the ball, also can adversely affect one's swing via messages received through the right hemisphere.

Golfers with such swings need not be treated as lepers, of course. All we're saying is you should avert your eyes while they perform their magic.

Improving your power to visualize

Here is a brief test which will gauge your present ability to visualize and at the same time provide you with a tool to increase that ability. Do it when you're relaxed, give yourself plenty of time to absorb each situation. Don't rush into answering the questions before you've completed your visualization.

Situation A

You are on a green at your home course. You have a six-foot downhill putt which breaks sharply to the left about three inches before it reaches the cup. Picture the green. Imagine yourself striking the ball and seeing it roll down the hill, take the break of the green and then go into the cup. Stop and visualize this shot to the best of your ability.

Then answer these questions:

(1) How hard was the putt struck—did it trickle into the hole or did it jam into the back of the cup?

(2) Did the ball roll true all the way to the hole or did it bounce during some part of its trip?

BONUS QUESTIONS:

(3) Was the green damp or dry?

On the same green with the same putt, imagine that your ball slid past the hole and ended up four feet past the cup on the low side. You are now faced with an uphill putt which breaks left to right about two inches.

(4) Can you see this putt in your mind's eye?

Situation B

You have placed your tee shot in the right rough on a hole which doglegs left to right. Consequently, you must hit a high fade over some trees which are blocking your approach to the green. You have chosen a 7-iron to hit this approach shot. Imagine your ball sailing over the corner trees and fading back in to touch down on the green. Close your eyes and see the entire shot. Now answer these questions:

(5) How close did your ball get to the trees at the closest point?

(6) Did your shot land pin high? Above the flag? Below the flag?

(7) Was there any wind blowing while your shot was in the air? If so, in what direction was it blowing?

(8) How many times did your ball bounce on the green?

(9) Did your ball bounce to the right? to the left? jump forward? suck backward?

BONUS QUESTIONS:

(10) What kind of trees were blocking your approach to the green?

Now imagine that you have driven in the left rough on a hole which doglegs right to left and has trees down the left side. You must hit a high hook to reach the green on this hole.

(11) Can you see this shot in your mind's eye?

Situation C

Your ball is lying in thick Bermuda rough about 20 feet from the green with a wide sand trap between the ball and the green. The hole is cut at the bottom of a slope about 15 feet from the edge of the trap, so you have very little green to work with and are going downhill. Imagine yourself lobbing the ball over the sand trap and seeing it trickling down the hill and stopping two feet from the cup. Now answer these questions.

(12) How close to the sand trap did your ball land?

(13) How many times did it bounce before it started rolling down the hill?

(14) Did your ball stop two feet short of the flag? Two feet past? To the right? To the left?

(15) About how high was your ball in the air at the apex of its flight?

BONUS QUESTIONS:

(16) What color was the flag on the flagstick?

Remove the sand trap and imagine that the cup is cut so that it is uphill from where your ball is lying, 20 feet away from the green in Bermuda rough. You are to hit a pitch shot to this flagstick.

(17) Can you see this shot in your mind's eye?

SCORING

Judge answers "correct" if you have formed a precise and positive image in your mind. If your original visualization has not taken into account the detail questioned, or if you saw something negative (for instance, your shot going into the bunker instead of on the green in Situation C), judge answers "incorrect."

If you answered questions 1, 2, 5, 6, 7, 8, 9, 12, 13, 14, 15 correctly, give yourself 5 points per question.

If you answered questions 3, 10, 16 correctly, give yourself 10 points per question.

Add up your total score. Maximum is 85. This is your score for *vividness of imagery ability.* If you scored below 70, you might consider working on this skill because it could help your shotmaking.

Now look at questions 4, 11 and 17. If you answered all three of these questions correctly, it probably means you have great *control* over your imagery. Some people can summon up vivid images in their mind, but they can't control what's going to be in the images, and that could mean trouble in golf. Research has shown that people who have both a high degree of vividness in their images and a great ability to control their imagery are the ones who can become most adept at physical skills.

10 KINESTHETIC SWING CUES

A teaching pro was trying to impart some basic swing information to a new pupil who was deaf. First, he wrote out various suggestions and directives on sheets of a legal pad, until his lesson tee was littered with good advice, but to no avail. Even with a demonstration it was obvious that they were getting nowhere fast. The pro decided to tell his pupil to just forget what they had done and come back in a couple of days. This time the pro put his hands on the pupil and manipulated him and the club into various key positions of the swing. The deaf person caught on right away.

Verbal cues and visual cues had failed, but kinesthetic cues—cues which worked directly on the pupil's right hemisphere, building up the correct swing feelings and actions in the INTEGRATOR through physical motion—did the job.

Instructors who place you or the club you are gripping into the correct positions on the lesson tee are teaching kinesthetically. A more sophisticated version of this approach is represented by the successful teaching program of PGA professional Paul Bertholy. Bertholy puts pupils through an exhaustive series of drills and exercises which gradually build up their golfing muscles, senses and the correct sequence of actions for making the swing. It's a little like basic training in the army, but it works for those golfers willing and able to make the effort required.

The golf swing can also be cued kinesthetically by some of the various swing-aid devices on the market and through your own exercise program.

Not all swing aids are beneficial or worth the price, nor are all exercises good for golf. Any exercises that build bulk in the upper arms and chest, for example, are bad because they tend to shorten your swing arc.

But some of the gadgets sold to help your game can be quite effective if used properly and regularly.

There's one called the Swing Expander that consists of a set of heavy cloth balls on an elasticized string. Swung correctly, it gives you the feeling of the centrifugal force you are trying to obtain in your golf swing.

There are also putting-track type devices which could possibly improve your putting mechanics, provided of course that you take the time to practice with them.

A few years ago LPGA teaching pro JoAnne Winter invented a grip aid that was intriguing, though it never sold well. It used a molded thermoplastic material in the shape of a golf grip. The golfer was to warm the material with his hands, then, under the direction of his teacher, place his hands in the correct grip. When he squeezed the warm material he made an imprint which became permanent. It could be used thereafter as a model of the correct grip sensation. It was a classic example of learning strictly by feel.

11 BETWEEN SHOTS—"COUNT SHEEP, NOT STROKES"

Time presents two special problems during the course of a round to the golfer trying to bridge the gap successfully from ANALYZER to INTEGRATOR:

—its vastness. Four or five hours of leisure in which the mind is unpegged from normal concerns and free to go anywhere.

—its finiteness. The very short brackets of time reserved for actual shotmaking, when the mind has to be ready to work at its very best.

Let's examine these problems briefly before turning to some psychological tools for improving shot execution itself.

An Olympic fencer named Paul Pesthy had a special method for coping with the time on his hands between matches. In fencing you don't have just one duel and call it a day. You must encounter a series of opponents over a long period.

Pesthy needed a way to get his mind off his previous match so he would be mentally fresh for the next one. Golfers face a similar situation in going from shot to shot in the course of playing a hole, and, on a larger scale, in going from hole to hole in the course of playing a round. In fact, golfers may lose more strokes in between shots, by mis-thinking and mis-feeling, than they do actually swinging the club, and it is mainly because of the special challenge the excess amount of time places on them.

Pesthy attacked the time problem by covering his head with a towel and imagined drawing an elaborate design of concentric circles, like a dartboard. This time-consuming exercise kept his mind occupied, preventing him from speculating on his lousy swordplay in the previous match or things that might go wrong in the upcoming match.

We can't literally put a towel over our heads

between shots on the golf course. But we can and should put our playing thoughts and concerns under wraps in some other way when it's not our turn to hit.

We saw Jack Nicklaus take part in all the usual banter in playing a pro-am at Inverrary in Florida a few years ago, yet he broke the course record. The laugh-a-minute format that developed from being paired with former President Ford, Bob Hope and Jackie Gleason did not keep Nicklaus from snapping back to attention when he had to and performing at his best on every shot.

Two logical sources of trivia to divert the mind in golf are the natural setting in which you find yourself and the other players in your group. They can keep you from dwelling on the wrong things between shots.

Contemplating nature is one of the most obvious pleasures in golf. Yet, it is often overlooked, especially by those so committed to excellence and improvement that anything that does not directly relate to their own game passes them by. If some of these self-ordained Hogans gave in to a little casual bird-watching between shots instead of brooding on their golf games, they'd probably play a lot better.

You don't have to be at Pebble Beach or Gleneagles to have access to natural wonders. Even on a flat, burnt-out, treeless nine-holer there is much in nature worth a look. Every golf course has a crow or two, a flowering bush, a pond or stream, the sky. There's something somewhere to look at, and as Yogi Berra once said, "You can observe a lot just by watching." That's one way to get the mind temporarily off your game.

Conversation with a friendly fellow golfer can also keep your mind properly diverted. Socializing with your playing partners is in fact an integral part of golf, and if you don't take any part in it, you're probably in the wrong sport. One psychologist has proposed that the camaraderie that develops among members of a foursome is akin to that experienced by mountain climbers or surfers. People play golf for the exercise and the competition. But they also develop a feeling of closeness with other golfers in the process of facing their common foe, the course, and this in itself becomes an important attraction in playing the game. That's why if you play golf with someone just once you'll often develop a greater affinity than if you had met in committee once a week or car-pooled together for a month.

In terms of the two-sided brain, these diversionary tactics work because they tend to keep your ANALYZER so involved in innocuous activity that it does not have a chance to engender overly technical considerations about the swing, nor permit the INTEGRATOR's emotional tendencies to get out of hand either.

In a similar manner, Harvard psychologists have cleverly reinterpreted the old advice about counting sheep to go to sleep.

It was always assumed that counting sheep made you think of quiet, pastoral things and lulled you to sleep. Or that the procedure was so inane and boring that you went to sleep in self-defense.

The real reason now appears to be that counting sheep keeps the left hemisphere so busy that the right hemisphere can't produce the irrational fears, anxieties and worries that traditionally keep people awake.

The operative word for golfers as far as choice of between-shot subjects goes is *innocuous*. Pick simple things to focus on. Working out tax deductions in your head between shots, or giving or taking advice on swing technique (unsolicited tips being the down side to the golfing camaraderie just mentioned) are examples of tasks that might be too complex for this purpose. The ANALYZER might get so involved in those subjects as to cause you to overlook an important detail about your next shot.

If you're socializing with other players, or scanning the environment for something to focus on, don't choose a topic or object that is apt to *arouse* your feelings. Just as overly complicated subjects will tend to distract the ANALYZER, overly controversial or stimulating subjects will confound the INTEGRATOR portion of your mind and make it harder for you to execute smoothly when the time comes to hit the ball.

Avoid talking about illness, for example, or some recent downturn or problem in your business life. Be aware of the debilitating effects of paying too much attention to something irritating or distracting around you. We play with a fellow who becomes exasperated by slow play. The moment he spots a slow-moving foursome, even if it's several holes ahead of him, his day is ruined, because he begins to project ahead to which hole he will eventually catch up with that group and there have his play held up. If we don't succeed in diverting him, we lose him and his playing ability to his obsession.

12 DURING SHOTS—THE 30-SECOND MORATORIUM

Johnny Miller once said the key to real concentration is being able to "focus in at a given time and then come out again." Lee Trevino may joke and chatter with the galleries, but he is similarly geared to the shot at hand whenever he sets up to his ball.

The depth and effectiveness that great players can reach in their concentration is impressive.

There's the famous story of Joyce Wethered playing a match at St. Andrews. She was putting for a crucial par on the 16th, which borders a railway line. A train came roaring by in the middle of her stroke, yet she sank the putt. After the match, she was asked if the train had bothered her, and she replied, "What train?"

That type of concentration can be developed but not forced. A club pro we know thought to inspire himself with the Wethered story when, stepping upon the first tee in the opening round of the Northwest Open, he heard a jet taking off from nearby Portland International Airport. As he addressed his tee shot the jet passed overhead. He swung the club, forced himself to think, "What plane? What plane?" The shot skittered off the toe 40 yards dead right.

The point is, you can't concentrate just by telling yourself to concentrate. But there are many ways to put yourself into that state of focused awareness that allows you to produce your best performance.

The first step is to designate the time frame during which this centering or focusing should occur.

Call a moratorium on chitchat and other irrelevant activities for about 30 seconds for every shot you face. Considered practically, this is not asking a lot. Thirty seconds a shot, with a bit more time thrown in for reading tricky greens and debating a prickly club-selection question occasionally, adds up to less than an hour of full concentration for the round if you hit the ball 100 times and little more than a half-hour if you shoot in the low 70's.

If you can concentrate this long for every shot, you'll be able to draw on your ANALYZER to do all the pre-shot analysis necessary, and to hand over control to your INTEGRATOR, which has the image and feeling of your good swing, when the moment comes to start the club back. In fact, this is how we would define good concentration in golf.

LPGA touring pro Jan Stephenson suggests thinking about each shot as a "mini-tournament in itself" as a way of intensifying your concentration. Imagine that you're carrying a clock that governs this ability to link the hemispheres properly in pure concentration, something like the clock chess players use to keep track of the time it takes them to decide on their moves during championships. When your time comes to set up for a shot, start the clock. Concentrate, à la chess champion Boris Spassky, and play your shot. Then turn the clock off. Start the clock again when your next shot is at hand. And so on through the round.

The 30-second moratorium helps lock the golfer into the here-and-now. It protects you from the various internal distractions which cause unnecessary focusing on things from the past or things in the future. And it protects you from external distractions—the various sights and sounds all around, including other golfers—which might be said to lead you away from your shot *in space.* If you hear a golf cart rumble over a bridge in a neighboring fairway, your mind flies to the noise. If your partner cries, "I can't believe this lie!" your mind immediately joins him in the woods.

We know it is possible to shut out such distractions because good golfers do it all the time. There is within the nervous system a gating mechanism that filters extraneous stimuli. If you're looking for a gas station on a busy road, you don't notice all the signs along the way or even all the gas station signs;

your mind may close the gates to everything except the sign of the gas station you have a charge card for. That's your only relevant stimulus at the moment.

Similarly, good golfers put their gating mechanism to work from the moment they have the club of their choice in hand and for the length of time it takes to hit their shots.

It's next to impossible to totally concentrate for the four or five hours it takes to finish a round of golf. Anyone who tries it starts to become mentally and physically drained by the fifth or sixth tee and feels more tension than he started with.

Yet, setting up to hit a golf shot without concentrating at all is just as futile. Indeed, it would be dangerous if your life depended on the outcome, for the golf swing is every bit as complex a motor skill as is any trapeze artist's double-flip. If golfers concentrated as well as acrobats must to avoid broken necks, more balls would end up in the short grass, on the fairway. The 30-second time frame establishes a specific limited interval in which to do it.

13 APPLYING THE "SOMATOPSYCHIC EFFECT" FOR BETTER SHOT EXECUTION

Most of us have heard of the psychosomatic effect—that behavioral syndrome in which the mind influences the body in some way. Usually it is mentioned in relation to health problems. Ulcers, hiatal hernias and hypertension are 20th century physical ills often brought about by mental stress.

You needn't have a sickness to experience its physiological consequences, though. Walk through a dark cemetery at night, contemplate some ghostly shadows, call to mind an Edgar Allan Poe story or one of the latest horror flicks, and presently your pulse will go up and you'll begin to breathe harder. No one's in the graveyard with you, but you have created mental threats to your safety, and this in turn has affected your body's machinery.

Hypnosis works in a similar way. If under hypnosis, a person becomes convinced he is sitting on an iceberg, he will develop goose bumps even though he is sitting in a 75-degree room.

Of more direct interest to golfers is the fact that this syndrome can also work in reverse, as a *somatopsychic effect.* In other words, the body can influence the mood of the mind. You may already be aware of this. If you ever exercised your body by swimming or jogging before an important meeting, you may have noticed that, during the actual meeting, you were more relaxed and could think more clearly and quickly.

Golf is not an action-reaction sport. It is a game in which every stroke starts from a dead standstill. This requirement to initiate the activity makes it easier for *physical* tension to creep in than it would in sports like tennis, basketball or soccer, where tension is often relieved simply through movement. And since golf is a game in which there is a lot of time between actual shotmaking activities, *mental* tension can be more easily aroused, too.

But it matters little whether the source of the tension is physical or mental, for the end result of either is invariably tension of both mind and body.

Using the phenomenon of the somatopsychic relationship—that influence of body upon mind—you can reverse this procedure. In golf there are three especially effective ways to remove tension on the physical level, so that mental tension is also dissipated:

—through a *pre-round routine* of warm-up drills, which helps the body make a smoother transition from off-course activities to golf;

—through a fixed *pre-shot routine*, which keeps the body in a more relaxed state before every shot; and

—through a *rehearsal-swing routine*, which helps the body stay relaxed on all those short shots and trouble shots that intrinsically produce nervousness.

Let's look at all three more closely.

The pre-round routine

Physical warm-up on the range prior to play is an accepted practice in major-league golf. Ninety percent of the pros do it; ninety percent of the amateurs do not. The irony is that a touring pro could crawl out of the trunk of an MG in Minot, North Dakota, in February, having slept in the car all night, and still hit an opening drive 275 yards straight down the fairway.

Needless to say, most of us can't do that. Even after two quick passes at a cigar butt or a dandelion, we can't execute our best swing on the first tee. In fact, we can't even *think* our best swing in the condition in which most of us usually arrive to play a round. If we lead busy lives, we've probably had to juggle half a dozen things in our business and family affairs to get out to the course in the first place. When we get to the first tee, we are often still behind the steering wheel of our car, physiologically and psychologically. We can't imagine the good swing very convincingly, nor can we execute it.

This might not be so bad if we gave ourselves the first few holes to "warm up" and didn't pay too much attention to the mis-hits we produced early in the round. But the ANALYZER in us does pay attention and starts trying to figure out where and how our swing mechanics have failed us.

Once again, we are failing our swing mechanics. That is, we are not giving ourselves a chance to play as well as we know how to play, because of poor psychology.

A good pre-round warm-up routine can solve that problem. Specifically, through some made-for-golf drills and a couple of simple exercises to relax the mind, a good routine can give the INTE-GRATOR a fighting chance to perform decently from the start, for the sake of the decent performance itself, and also to prevent the ANALYZER from getting prematurely overactive.

Numerous drills and exercises have been devised by instructors to help players get their golfing muscles limber in lieu of loosening up by hitting balls—certainly the best method—and to promote the rhythm and coordination appropriate to the game. For example:

> Hold your driving club parallel to the ground in front of you at waist level, hands spread to shoulder width, palms facing downward. Raise the club over your head and pull it down across and brace it against your back just below your neck. Turn your body using your shoulders and legs as you would for the golf swing. Do a series of these turns, gradually working the club down your back, loosening your back muscles as you go.

If you try this exercise, you'll notice it makes you feel much more extension in your arms when you set up to the ball. Your arms will seem to be "hanging" more from your shoulders; the muscles won't feel bunched up as if you were still fighting traffic.

It's up to you, the individual golfer, to choose the particular exercises you want to do, but remember that the purpose of any of them will be the same — to make you feel like you're ready for hitting your driver, instead of for driving your car.

If you do have a few moments but can't get to the range, stroke some putts across the green toward no particular target, just to get a relaxed feel.

Hit a few practice putts with your eyes shut. Lee Trevino recommends doing this because it removes the anticipation of the hit from the mind and so fosters smoother stroking.

Hit a few chips or pitches without looking to check the direction of the shots. Keep your ANALYZER out of it. Just try to put a right-hemisphere feeling on the stroke itself.

Then do the stretching drill mentioned, followed by some slow, lazy practice swings with your eyes shut. It's a great way to get in touch with what your body feels like this particular day.

As you're doing the exercises, zero in on your basic swing cues. Mentally rehearse your pre-shot routine a couple of times before going to the tee. Picture a good tee shot you've hit before on this hole, or on one like it if it's a strange course. Your mind needs to be warmed up as much as your body.

Though this "mental practice" is not strictly somatopsychic in nature, it belongs as part of the pre-round routine. Conceivably, as research and experience on new potential applications of the mind in sports continue, the time may come when mental practice alone will almost be sufficient as preparation for performance. Already some golfers have claimed it works quite well for them at times — Pat Fitzsimons used to like to sit under a tree and work on his game in his mind prior to playing a tournament round.

In any case, the end result of a good pre-round routine is an INTEGRATOR that's been fine-tuned for the job of teeing off. Even if you have only five minutes to devote to the routine, that result is well worth going after.

The pre-shot routine

All the pros follow a fixed pre-shot routine—a ritual of thoughts and actions that includes checking the lie, checking wind conditions, visualizing the shot, selecting the club, sighting the target area, gripping the club, lining up in relation to the target and setting up to the ball. Some do it quickly, like Lee Trevino or Lanny Wadkins, others work more methodically, like Nicklaus. But they all do it.

Top golfers take the trouble to do this, yet three out of four amateur golfers, we would estimate, do not, at least not with the same regularity. The tasks involved aren't very challenging athletically or intellectually and may even seem trivial. That's probably why so many weekend golfers fail to see the value of some regular countdown to contact.

For the pros, the pre-shot routine is, above all, a way of ensuring better mechanics. It gives the ANALYZER a chance to figure out what has to be done before the INTEGRATOR does its thing. The pros may use their ANALYZER at this time to checklist basics of grip, stance and alignment and to evaluate other factors that may influence the shot, much as the airplane pilot goes through his pre-flight checklist. What kind of lie do I have? How far is it? Is there any wind? Where's the trouble?

This procedure in itself reduces tension and indecision. By ordering all the minor mental and physical tasks to be done before the swing, the routine makes it unlikely that any piddling, unexpected or forgotten detail will crop up after the ANALYZER has handed over control of the swing to the INTEGRATOR.

In the absence of a routine, the ANALYZER has to go into overdrive to sort out the variables placed before it. If you stand up to the ball, then set your club down for one shot and reverse that sequence on the next shot, you give the mind an unnecessary adaptation job. Without an established routine, you'll tend to feel like you're re-inventing the wheel every time you step up to swing.

For most players, the pre-shot routine is probably even more valuable for psychological reasons than it is for mechanical reasons. Without the same thoroughly grooved repeating action that the pros have achieved in their swings through countless practice hours, amateur players are naturally more susceptible to doubt and insecurity about their swings at the start. But by patterning your pre-shot behavior properly, you can reduce the chances of those negative thoughts and feelings from surfacing.

The pre-shot routine reduces tension somatopsychically. It builds habits that the body begins to recognize and eventually to welcome. Moving into familiar positions and doing things in familiar patterns breeds the feeling of physical well-being that in turn promotes a sense of security in the mind. When the body is put through the same motions prior to every shot and comes to recognize those motions and feel comfortable with them, it's much easier to stay relaxed yet be sharp mentally.

It also reduces tension by putting your mind on the routine and keeping it off the *results* of the upcoming shot. By going about its business, the ANALYZER keeps the right hemisphere from taking the stage prematurely—for example, by imagining an unrealistically good or bad shot. Tension creeps into the swing when you're trying for your career 7-iron or when you're fearful you may hook the ball into a pond. If the ANALYZER didn't keep busy, the INTEGRATOR's emotional side might be able to assert itself with such notions more easily.

Among the touring pros there's a great variety in the rituals they use to get mind and body ready to perform. Some players assume their stance right foot first, for example, others with both feet together. Some players sole the club behind the ball, others suspend it in the air.

Certain pre-swing mannerisms are the function of different swing styles. For example, left-side-dominant, strong leg players such as Tom Watson tend to address the ball more toward the heel of the club. That's because they're going to be coming from inside the line on the downswing. Right-sided hand players tend to address the ball off the toe of the club, because they throw the club a bit more away from them on the downswing.

There's no single pre-shot routine suitable for all golfers, but once you establish your own routine, stick to it religiously. Once during a practice session a fellow pro tried to get Tom Weiskopf to shorten his routine by five seconds, thinking it might help his game, but Weiskopf couldn't produce his normal shots from a quicker setup. As soon as his well-meaning friend went away, he went back to his natural pattern.

The final act in the pre-shot routine is to trigger the swing without undue delay. Most golfers use some kind of tension-reducing forward press to get the swing under way physically. Mentally, it can be launched with a swing cue. After you've done all you can do in your setup, the idea is to switch control to your INTEGRATOR—to get into your right hemisphere as quickly and smoothly as you can. If you haven't "taken away" your ANALYZER by the time of your takeaway, you're in trouble.

For at this point, it's up to the INTEGRATOR side of your brain to make it happen. No further contributions from the left hemisphere are needed and, in most cases, would be disruptive—as disruptive, say, as interrupting someone in the middle of knotting a necktie. Supplying that key word or word-picture provokes the INTEGRATOR to re-experience the feeling of the good golf swing—so that the body in turn can execute the swing that matches that feeling. Once that stimulus is provided, the ANALYZER should stand back and shut up. Said Julius Boros once, "The middle of your swing is no time to give yourself a lesson."

Some people have argued that you should have nothing on your mind when you start your swing. Actually, it's doubtful if a "blank mind" can really exist. Even under hypnosis the brain is busy. We think most golfers would be better off to cue the swing with one specific thought or picture. This not only makes it easier to initiate a good swing in total, but the presence of the cue or image itself tends to block out the extraneous thoughts and feelings that a fertile mind will surely produce once it sees the field is clear.

The rehearsal swing routine

We've concentrated on the preparation required for the full shot. The somatopsychic effect has a special application on all trouble shots, short shots and putts—strokes that require more confidence and right-hemisphere feel for the distance you want the ball to go.

On anything within 75 yards of the green, on the green itself and for any extra-challenging shot from an unusual lie, a bad position or over an imposing hazard, *rehearse* the stroke you're going to make at least two or three times as part of your pre-shot routine.

Touring pros, you'll notice, seldom take more than one practice swing prior to driving, and some of them won't even do that. They've made the full swing a few hundred thousand times and are pretty sure it's going to be there when they call for it.

But watch the pros when they have to play a difficult in-between shot near the green. On tricky pitches, chips and putts, some players will take several swings before actually stepping up to the ball.

Rehearsing the swing allows you to relate your objective view of the distance required to a subjective feeling for the length and firmness of stroke that will produce a shot going that distance.

At the same time, it puts mind and body in a more confident state regarding the outcome of the shot.

Suppose you have a pitch shot over a bunker to the green. If you rehearse the stroke a few times with short practice swings so that you feel the precise length and firmness you'll need to get the ball near the cup, your body will be more relaxed when you step up to execute it. If your body feels sure, it will create a sureness of mind that in turn will let the body do what it is really capable of doing.

What is likely to happen if you don't rehearse the swing for your short pitch?

On the actual shot, if you take the club back too far, your INTEGRATOR will sense you're going to over-hit and arrange for the club to decelerate on the way down—so that you stub the ball into the bunker.

Or if you don't take the club back far enough, the INTEGRATOR will think "more power!" and make you swing forward over-enthusiastically— probably causing you to top the shot or pull it sharply.

When actors rehearse for a play, they don't worry about getting their lines right the first time. They try to get a feel for the character they're portraying and for the flow of the play. Part of the purpose of the rehearsal-swing routine for golfers is to experiment, too—to edit out the mistakes in swing length or firmness of stroke before it actually counts.

Some players when chipping go through this process before they actually set their club behind the ball. They might take too big a backswing on the first rehearsal stroke for the distance to be covered, too short a backswing on the next rehearsal stroke. Their INTEGRATOR tells them "too big," "too short." Then they'll dial in on something in between those extremes, until finally their INTEGRATOR says, "just right." Now they have the stroke to take on stage for opening night.

Rehearsing the stroke comes almost automatically on the greens, with visualization becoming crucial. One pro goes so far as to roll an imaginary ball up to the cup with his hand to be sure to get that right-hemisphere feeling for the distance to the cup. Then he'll incorporate that feeling into the putting stroke he's rehearsing. Finally, he'll putt.

High-pressure shots of any length can benefit from rehearsal. If you have to hit a fairway wood from a tight lie with water to clear, for example, it may not be enough for you to tune up for the shot with your usual waggle or practice swing. Maybe it will take two or three rehearsal swings to fully develop a physical feeling for the stroke—and with that, the mental confidence that you can do it. You're more likely to mis-fire if you are feeling the pressure and you'll try to make the shot without going through these special preliminaries.

14 APPLYING THE TRANSFER PRINCIPLE TO IMPROVE PLAY

It's usually easier to perform a skill better if your practice of the skill takes place under conditions that closely resemble the conditions that exist when the performance really counts.

Basketball coaches observe this principle, known to psychologists as the *transfer of identical elements*, when at the end of a workout they set the clock at three minutes and make their players practice free throws in situations which closely approximate late-game conditions. Sinking baskets under these conditions is what wins most games, not practicing shooting when relaxed and physically fresh.

There are three potentially important applications of this transfer principle in golf:
—practicing under playing conditions;
—overplaying nemesis holes;
—playing new courses like familiar layouts.

Practice under "game conditions"

Without the benefit of a coach to ride herd on us, we have to create our own "game conditions" in practice sessions in golf and also in social rounds. But it can be done. Except for the putting, you can play virtually every shot of an 18-hole round on the practice range if you take the time and effort to go about it, using your imaginative right hemisphere to create facsimiles of realistic settings for each shot. And what's wrong with putting out all those gimmes you tend to get when you're not playing for scores or stakes, by telling yourself each two-footer is for the club championship?

Bob Toski used to practice putting as a kid with three balls—one marked "Snead," one "Hogan" and one "Toski." By personalizing his work on the greens in this way, he added not only interest but competitive pressure to his practice routine.

When he practiced early in his career, Gary

Player made himself hole out five bunker shots before calling it a day. In this way, he forced the repetition that builds real consistency. He overlearned how to play out of sand—one of his greatest skills to this day. And he did it under competition-like pressure.

Jackie Burke developed his great consistency on the greens in the same way. He'd often skip the side bets with the other pros during practice rounds before a tournament and go off by himself to work on his short game instead. "I didn't come here to win a $20 Nassau," he once remarked. "I came to win the tournament." Sometimes Burke would make himself sink 100 three-foot putts in a row before quitting for the day. Some club golfers we know would be delighted to sink three three-foot putts in a row, of course, but the idea behind Burke's routine is sound and relevant in degree to all of us. It not only created great consistency in his putting stroke, but forced him to sink those last dozen putts or so under tremendous pressure—if he missed he had to start all over again.

We can put the same kind of pressure on ourselves not necessarily by holing out but by *getting* out of a bunker five times in a row, for instance, or by sinking 5 or 10 three-foot putts in a row, instead of an improbable 100. The more we experience the type of pressure relative to our own level of play, the less it will bother us when it comes up during actual matches.

This can be broadened to cover the playing of holes and not just shots. Tony Lema would imagine being in the British Open when he played his solitary rounds in Elko, Nevada, where he worked as a club pro at a nine-hole course before going on tour. He would create situations as he went along that made it seem as though the Open title he eventually did win depended upon making par or birdie.

When Johnny Miller was learning the game, his instructor, John Geertsen, would end each lesson by putting a ball down and saying, "John, this one is for the Masters. Hit that 75-yard sign out there."

And Miller would respond by bearing down, and he'd come close to hitting the sign every time.

Tom Watson used to conjure up an imaginary Jack Nicklaus to trade shots with on the practice tee. This exercise not only kept him alert for the length of his practice session, but may even have prepared him a bit better mentally for the specific task of outdueling Nicklaus at both the Masters and the British Open as he did so brilliantly in 1977.

Practice itself goes better if you work at it as though it's for real. But also, when you practice the way you play, you'll be more likely to play the way you practice.

If you can hit a series of shots from the practice bunker believing a championship depends upon each one of them, you'll be more likely to get it up and down from the sand when you really have to during a round.

That's not only because you will have worked on the skill required for the job. It's also from experiencing success under self-imposed pressure in these situations. If your imagery is good enough, you'll step up to the shot having "been there."

Overplay nemesis holes

Suppose, like many golfers, you have a particular nemesis hole on the course where you play most of your rounds. Most of us do. For some reason you can never score well on that hole, no matter what you try. You're psyched-out by the hole. It jinxes you. Every time you step on the tee to hit, you're flooded by negative thoughts and feelings.

Your problem is similar to that of a poor sand player who never practices sand shots. There's no way to get better unless you develop a pattern of success on the hole. And the way to do that is to experience success when it doesn't count, then transfer it when it does.

Go out some time when the course isn't crowded and play the problem hole with three or four balls. Play it over and over until you make your par or birdie. Then, if you can, repeat the good score a couple of times more.

It may not be possible to confront the nemesis hole directly in this manner on the course where you play. In that case, play it repeatedly on the practice tee. Use your right hemisphere to recreate the hole in your mind's eye, then play it the way it should be played. In other words, develop a pattern of success in a practice situation that you can transfer to the same hole in a playing situation.

Play new courses like familiar layouts

Another potentially valuable application of the theory of the transfer of identical elements comes when playing unfamiliar courses.

Many amateur golfers play almost exclusively at one course and get to know it so well they could walk it in their sleep. The trouble for them comes when they venture onto new turf, as on vacation or during a local tournament held somewhere else. The fear of the unknown, common to all of us, manifests itself on these occasions, sometimes in the form of exaggerated notions about the *length* of each hole on a strange course, and the prodigious shot-making required to make any of the greens in regulation.

Golfers in new surroundings may try to put something extra on their swings, quickening their tempo and hitting from the top or jumping at the ball.

Next time you face a new golfing challenge, try translating the holes on that layout into the holes that most closely resemble them on your home course. Then play your familiar holes. If the first hole on the unfamiliar course is a straightaway 375-yard, par 4, mentally review the holes on your home course for its lookalike, then picture and retrieve the swing you use on that hole for your model for the swing you need now.

Not every new hole will be a perfect match but the strangeness in the vast majority of them can be tamed and so made easier to play psychologically.

15 PRACTICE SESSION PSYCHOLOGY

Practice makes permanent, not perfect. If you are determined and willing to work on your game, let your sessions be governed by these three simple learning principles:

—"over-practice" what you're trying to learn;
—space your practice sessions at regular intervals;
—make sure you practice the right things.

Overlearning

In all the motor skills research that has been done over the years—much of it motivated by the desire to get maximum performance out of the individual, whether on the assembly line or the Olympic team—the single most valid procedure for learning that has emerged has been overlearning or repetition of the correct response.

A simple motor skill such as touch-typing is developed through drills. After you have depressed the "q" key with your little finger a couple of thousand times, in the course of doing these drills, you can be pretty sure of beginning the word "quiet" without making an error.

A complex motor skill like golf is developed similarly. Overlearning involves reaching goals— for example, landing twenty 7-iron shots within 15 feet of a practice flag—and then practicing even beyond that goal. The shots hit after reaching the goal are the overlearning shots.

To overlearn, you must be selective about what you're working on. If you divide a practice hour into six 10-minute sessions devoted to (1) driving, (2) fairway woods, (3) sand shots, (4) chipping, (5) putting and (6) long-iron shots, you're not going to overlearn anything. Even if you devote the entire hour to the full swing, but divide it into (1) setup, (2) takeaway, (3) position at the top, (4) downswing,

(5) contact and (6) finish, you may not overlearn anything.

It usually takes time and repetition to drum into your INTEGRATOR the specific swing action or shotmaking knack you're after. That means keeping the focus sharp and specific throughout the practice session.

"Beating balls" is the tried-and-true version of overlearning in golf. It's what might be termed the excellence-by-quantity method. There's also an excellence-by-quality method. If the *quality* of your concentration, involvement, mental imagery and swing feel is high, then you can achieve good results hitting fewer balls.

Learning at intervals

A lot of studies have shown that people learn better in relatively short sessions that take place at regular intervals, rather than in once-a-month marathon workouts.

You're better off practicing chipping for 10 minutes a day for several days, for example, than devoting a single two-hour session during the week to the job.

Overextended practice sessions promote boredom, experimentation or taking the task too lightly, any and all of which can lead to learning the wrong things. We know many putters who've come away from self-imposed, gruelingly long workouts on the practice green with different and worse strokes than the ones they started with. They failed to recognize the pitfalls that one can encounter during excessive practice.

Learning what you want to learn

It's easy to overlearn the wrong thing in golf because the feedback can be ambiguous. If you stroke the wrong key in typing, your mistake stands out at once, so you can change your behavior to prevent it from happening again. In golf you can make a bad stroke and not realize it. The outside-in type swing productive of wild slices doesn't necessarily feel bad or wrong to a novice golfer. And should he see one out of 10 of his banana balls land in the fairway, it may even suggest to him that the swing is fine and that some other factor, possibly the wind, blew the rest of the shots off line. The occasional random payoff that keeps gamblers glued to slot machines keeps many golfers swinging in the same incorrect manner.

The cure for this is to develop objective feedback to guide you during your practice sessions. That's why a teaching professional, or at least someone whom you trust with a good eye for the game, comes in handy.

That's also why the practice tees along the tournament circuit are usually strewn with golf clubs being used as directional guides. They provide a form of *objective* feedback for the pros, allowing the players to see for themselves whether they're lined up straight. The greatest golfers in the world worry about such things, because they've found out through experience that it's easy to learn when you want to learn. Even top-ranking professionals have a hard time recognizing alterations and compensations they make trying to keep their games tuned to a weekly test. That's why pros have pros.

When to forget practice

There's something to be said for *not practicing* at times. Most often that would be when you're tired or in a deep slump.

If your game is way off the mark, all you may do in a practice session is reinforce the erroneous patterns in your play. Or you may make unnecessary changes in your technique.

Some top pros will practice after a round in the 60's but not after one in the 80's. When they've got the good feeling, they don't want to let it go. They try to prolong their effectiveness by keeping the good swing as fresh as possible in their right hemispheres.

If you're really mis-swinging, it may be a good idea to stop playing or practicing for a while and let the interference fall away. That will happen if your bad habits are not so firmly ingrained as the good habits they have somehow temporarily replaced. After an absence, and without any conscious effort, you may find you're once again swinging the way you want to. You're more relaxed. Your ANALYZER isn't bombarding you with swing details, so your INTEGRATOR can function more smoothly again.

When to remember practice

A really good practice session doesn't have to end with the last swing. If you've been hitting the ball well or performing the shot that you set out to practice with exceptional accuracy and consistency, that session can become a kind of data bank of golf-appropriate responses for your INTEGRATOR to draw on in the future.

Prior to the Masters one year, Bert Yancey had a practice session like that, and he intuitively stored it for reference later on.

"I was hitting the ball as pure as I ever will," he recalled. "Thereafter, when I was someplace else and trying to get my swing right, I'd project myself to that Augusta tee and I'd begin to hit better. It was an intangible thing, but it worked."

16 KEEPING A GAME JOURNAL

None of us is smart enough to remember everything we know. That's why we think most golfers would benefit from keeping some kind of record of their experience in play and practice—an informal log, notebook or journal, like the one on pages 84-85.

It doesn't have to be kept with the zeal of a C.P.A. or in any particular format. We have one friend who uses his golf bag as his game journal. The bag is covered with dozens of little plastic labels stamped with words like "Low 'n slow" and "Think smoooooth"—our friend's kine swing cues.

Storing verbal or visual swing cues is one good use for a game journal. As we said earlier, writing those cues down when you're playing at your best is the only sure way to remember them later on. Those cues won't trigger the correct swing for you every time, nor will they work for you indefinitely. But sometimes you can return to an old cue and find it has regained its power to elicit the good swing.

The journal can also be used to record the results of your practice sessions. Suppose you are practicing chip shots to a specific target area in your yard or at the range. Use the journal to write down the number of shots that finish within the circle. Do this every time you practice chip shots. Soon you'll have solid data about your chipping skill. Practice will improve your chipping strokes, but by itself it may not give you the confidence to execute the shots well during actual play. If, however, you've read in your journal that you are consistently hitting 20 out of 25 within the target area, almost nothing can prevent you from believing in your chipping ability during a round.

Use the game journal to set goals for yourself. When you focus on a measurable objective in positive terms, you have a much better chance of making progress than if you merely go out and "try hard" or throw yourself willy-nilly into some self-improvement program.

March 20

* Putting excellent. Can feel distance 1/2 way 2/3 then roll ball dead into hole — push blade toward target — pick which side of hole you want ball to enter. RHYTHM !

March 25

Shot 77-73 Understanding Importance of Plane. More weight left to reduce fluffed chips + pitches. * Keep hands out of chip when close to flag — like putt.

March 26

Experimented with stronger left-hand grip and more closing of clubface in solid position as cure for pushing long irons —
Completely screwed up !

April 2

Keep the blade more square going back on wedge — don't fan face — just let wrists cock — SLOW — SMOOTH
Think the ball right where you want it to go. Hogan's concentration. Ward's determination. Mentally rehearse your upcoming shot.

April 4

Shot 70 at E.C.C. from white tees. Irons much better. Missed shot when didn't do routine or didn't trust my position.

Work more on feeling distance
  with wedge ...
Need more putting practice ...
Woods - close face more at address —
  stay on inside approaching ball.
ONE SHOT AT A TIME!

April 5
    Shot 33 at Oakway on front. Need
to play less break on greens when wet—
take a little more time on your read—

April 10   Pro-Am + Race Horse - Shadow Hills
    Be ready when its time to tee up —
arrive early enough so not rushed—
    Make good decisions from tee when
odds dictate on driving holes—
    TAKE YOUR TIME UNDER PRESSURE
TO THINK OUT AND VISUALIZE SHOT!

April 13
    Still leaving ball right —
    Moved ball forward - no help
    Tried very upright swing - feels bad.

April 14   Played Illahe C.C. - bad weather
    Shot 78 - 5 penalty shots! Took too
many chances with little to gain—
    STUPID. Some good irons taking
away on line of flight not inside

April 15 Played nine with juniors. Hit
ball awful, still shot 35 on front. Grip
not good. Had to force face shut—stance
too open, not natural.

Motivation always becomes more deeply rooted when goals are stated in concrete terms or when deadlines are assigned for attaining them. Organizations like Alcoholics Anonymous and Weight Watchers depend on the power of the individual's articulation of goals to bring about behavior changes. True, it may be easier to go on the wagon or shed 20 pounds than it is to play 18 holes without a three-putt, but writing down positive goals in itself may actually bring them closer to realization.

The game journal doesn't have to be limited to material related to the mental, emotional or psychological side of the game. It's also a logical place to record your scores, tactical information about different holes and courses, and notes on mechanics and techniques.

PART III
PERSONALITY AND ATTITUDES

17 SHIELDING THE TWO-HEMISPHERE GAME

Tournament Day, Finals:

Only 15 minutes to go before I tee off in this big match. Isn't there a level lie anywhere on this range? Got to get that lousy tail off the drive. Better not hit any more practice balls, I haven't putted yet. Well, just one more. Good Lord, that'd be O.B. on the first hole. Hit another, you can't go to the tee with that shot on your mind. Keep your wrist flat, stupid. Ah, that's better, a little draw. Where did all these people come from? You'd think it was the U.S. Open. Maybe I should hit a 4-wood for openers just to keep it in play. C'mon, where's your guts? Think positively! YOU CAN DO IT—that's better.

Why am I so nervous? I know almost everyone here. They're all my friends . . . well, most of them are. Snoopy was right; "Happiness *is* getting off the first tee on Sunday with a lot of people standing around."

I've been lucky to get this far . . . even in the second flight . . . two forfeits didn't hurt. Jim breezed right through. He *ought* to be in the championship flight . . . sandbagged the qualifying. Now it's him and me.

C'mon, quit leaving the ball short on these putts. That's what Snead says happens when you're choking. "Never up, never in." Whoa, not that far by! I wonder which putter I should

PERSONALITY AND THE TWO-SIDED BRAIN

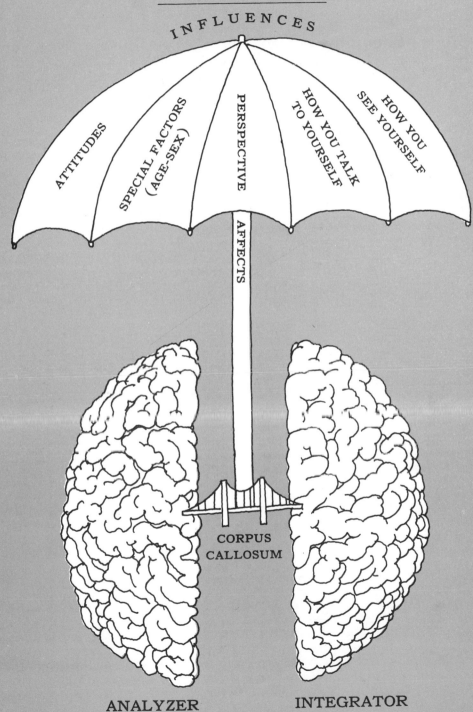

PERSONALITY

INFLUENCES

ATTITUDES

SPECIAL FACTORS (AGE-SEX)

PERSPECTIVE

HOW YOU TALK TO YOURSELF

HOW YOU SEE YOURSELF

AFFECTS

CORPUS CALLOSUM

ANALYZER

INTEGRATOR

take? Could the greens be this slow on the course? Do you suppose they forgot to cut the practice green?

They're calling my name. Five minutes to go. Why did they have to get a loudspeaker? Didn't warm up enough. . . . Should have gotten here earlier. Should have hit a few bunker shots. Should have done my yoga. Should have. . . .

Oh, no! There's my sister and her loudmouthed boyfriend. Don't tell me they're going to follow the match! He'll try to talk to me the whole round.

Geez, I forgot to buy long tees. Now I *better* use the 4-wood. "Excuse me, coming through, yeah, thanks, I'll need a little luck."

"Jim, nice to see you. Yeah, great day for golf." (Damn this wind) "Hope you have a good round too, Jim." (No, I don't) "Anyway, let's just go out and have some fun and add 'em up, it really isn't that important." (Oh, yes, it is) "I'm up first? Great!" (Awful. My hands are shaking. . . .)

Earlier in this book we described the kind of left- and right-hemisphere activity that contributes to smooth and consistent shot execution in golf. But what evidence of constructive activity can you find in the inner monologue of the golfer given above?

Hardly any. "Keep your wrist flat, stupid," might pass for an act of the ANALYZER—but not a very helpful one.

The overwhelming impression created by this monologue is that of an individual preoccupied by a lot of practical and social concerns. It is a *personal-*

ity that we hear, not the two-hemisphere golf brain at work. In this case, a personality is making it all but impossible for a golf-appropriate ANALYZER/ INTEGRATOR relationship to take place.

To put it another way, suppose that you have an important chip to make from the fringe. Your ANALYZER studies the situation and says, "I see the line!"

Good. Now your INTEGRATOR takes a few rehearsal swings and says, "I feel the distance!"

Fine. But now one more vote has to be counted. One more voice has to be heard before you can really make a good chip. In some form, your personality has to declare: "I can knock the ball right into the hole!"

In our view, the personality serves as a kind of giant umbrella influencing and affecting the ANALYZER/INTEGRATOR mind work we described earlier. The star of our monologue was someone whose umbrella was actually closed—his personality offered him no protection whatsoever from doubt, indecision, negativism, or competitive jitters.

In this section, we hope to show ways in which the golfer can create out of his or her own personality the best possible umbrella for aiding the two-hemisphere game.

18 SELF-CONCEPT ON THE COURSE

Some aspects of the personality may lie outside our total control. Others are of our own making. These are the ones we should concentrate on because there is room for change here—if, indeed, change would help improve our performance on the golf course.

The single most important aspect of personality within our means to change is the ongoing portrait we sketch of ourselves as golfers—how we see ourselves and how highly we value what we see.

A good deal of research has been done to show that a positive self-concept and a high self-esteem are related to better achievement, academically and athletically. Indeed, the best students are not always the ones with the most brains, and the best jocks are not necessarily those gifted with the most strength, speed or natural coordination.

In other words, even if you have the equipment to be a fine golfer, your game may suffer if you allow yourself to slip into a negative mode of thinking and feeling.

"When I play with someone like Jack Nicklaus, I just feel like I am in the way," a young pro remarked one year at the Masters. He had just shot quite a respectable second-round 71 but, upon learning that he would be paired with Nicklaus for the third round, he made the comment that revealed in what little esteem he held himself as a player at that particular time. Next day he shot 81 and was out of contention.

Let's look at a few actual shot situations in which golfers allowed a poor or erroneous self-concept to cost them strokes.

"The club pro joined us on the second hole just as I addressed a long 3-iron. My normal shot is a slice, but I didn't want the pro to think I was a slicer because I know the slice is regarded as the weaker shot. So I told myself, 'Don't let it slice to the right!' And I didn't—I pulled it into the trap on the left side of the green."

This player's normal shot—the slight fade—probably would have gone on the green, but the arrival of the pro prompted him to try to change his image. All of a sudden he was more concerned with what someone thought than the result of the shot. But his INTEGRATOR didn't know how to produce the shot required.

"In the last round of a tournament, I flew the ninth green and my ball hit a cart path and rolled some 40 yards through the galleries. It went around a corner and rolled to a stop under the scorer's table. I could have taken a free drop to a nice grassy area that would have given me a shot at the green, but I was so embarrassed I hit it from there and got away as fast as I could."

The player, a professional, ordinarily knew the rule permitting him a free drop, but his self-concept would not permit him to accept the amateurish shot and resulting bad luck he had had, so he lost his composure and at least one stroke.

"I had joined the club and was playing in my first member-guest. On the first hole my ball landed on the front edge of the U-shaped green, but my line to the pin was blocked by an intervening sand trap. I was so nervous about playing acceptably and not desecrating the greens, I couldn't think straight. Instead of putting away from the hole around the hazard, or taking a wedge and chipping over it to the pin, I stroked my ball directly into the sand."

The player felt that his self-concept was really on the line this day to begin with, and when he found himself in that spot on the first green, his normal reasoning powers fled. He putted into the bunker as though it were the socially acceptable thing to do—which was like committing suicide just to be polite.

Apropos of that situation, the great British player, Henry Cotton, one year stunned the sedate Open galleries at Sandwich in England by using a wedge on a huge green instead of a putter and gouging a healthy divot out of the turf as he did so. Heavy rains, he explained later, had made the greens extremely slow and he decided it was easier to get his ball to the pin with the wedge than to try putting it some 80 feet. Cotton's self-concept wasn't affected by what the fans might have thought, so his imagination was free to deal with the shot on its own terms.

"While on a trip and playing with borrowed clubs of a pro friend of mine, I came to where I needed to hit a short approach. I decided I would play a 9-iron instead of a pitching wedge because I wasn't happy with the pitching wedge in my own set of clubs at home and I was afraid of using the borrowed wedge. Anyway, I set up to my shot just when my friend arrived on the scene. He asked me what I was hitting and suddenly I realized I had pulled a 6-iron out of the bag. As I went back to my bag, he commented that knowing the difference between the 6 and 9 is the first lesson in golf. Then as I re-addressed my shot, he asked me why I wasn't using a pitching wedge. I explained all that and finally hit the

9-iron and to no one's surprise, it went
all of 10 yards."

Notice how in this case the golfer's self-concept
gets worse by stages:

The borrowed clubs feel strange.

The pitching wedge in the borrowed clubs re-
minds him of how badly he plays with his own
pitching wedge.

The 6-iron he mistakenly pulls out makes him
feel stupid.

The pro's remark about the difference between
the 6-iron and 9-iron makes him feel silly.

The pro's questioning his using the 9-iron instead of the wedge makes him feel like he doesn't
know how to play approach shots.

By this time he doesn't.

The negative self-fulfilling prophecy is the most
dramatic example of how a poor self-concept and
low self-esteem invariably lead to mediocre performance on the golf course.

After he won the PGA Championship, Al
Geiberger went for eight years without winning another tournament. Later he analyzed this victory
drought as follows:

"I didn't win for such a long time that I built up
a negative barrier. It was a trap I set for myself. I
went into tournament after tournament thinking
that the best I could do was make the cut and maybe
earn a little money."

Geiberger thought he was lucky just to be making the cut every week, and his performance did not
rise above the level of that expectation. Eventually,
it did—he broke out of his slump with several vic-
tories, including the one at Memphis in 1977
during which he carded a historic 59.

We tend to do as well or as poorly as we expect to
do partly because the expectation itself affects performance but, more importantly, because it fosters
changes in our behavior which pave the way for
that anticipated performance.

A golfer thinks he's a poor sand player. Not poor

for the reason that he doesn't own a sand iron, or has never taken a lesson on bunker shots, or doesn't practice—but just born to be inept out of the sand. With this expectation, the golfer avoids taking lessons or practicing because he knows it won't do any good. When he does get into a bunker, he rushes to get out—because he knows he's going to have to do it twice. Anyway, he fails, and this confirms his expectation of being a poor sand player and keeps him in a vicious circle about the problem.

This syndrome isn't unique to golfers, or to sports in general. Take the student who thinks he's a dunce in math. He'll flunk math tests as often as the fellow in the previous example skulls sand shots. That's because he won't prepare for the tests by studying ("What good will studying do? I don't have the aptitude for math"), or by asking for help on points he doesn't understand. ("It's not the teacher's fault or the textbook's fault. I just don't get math.") And when the time comes for exams, he'll tense up and probably keep what knowledge he has managed to acquire about math a state secret.

The self-fulfilling prophecy can take root within the framework of an individual shot as well as in more general skill areas such as putting or sand play or math. Again, however, the negative expectations alone do not produce negative results. The expectations must also give rise to some kind of inappropriate behavior—rushing the backswing, say, or hitting from the top—before the mis-hit shot results.

Once the bad forecast translates into bad news, the real damage is done, because the mis-hit shots that result tend to prove the bad forecast was right and will generate new bad forecasts.

The negative self-fulfilling prophecy is easier to put into effect than the positive one simply because in golf, as in any discipline, there are always many more opportunities to fail than there are to succeed. In other words, if you *think* you're the world's worst putter, you'll *become* one of the world's worst putters, because there are dozens of different ways to miss every putt you face.

If you think you're the world's *best* putter, however, that forecast won't hold *unless* the perceptions you make are translated into some specific action designed to support your claim. If you make 15 putts in a row from two feet on the practice green for 10 days in a row, your putting forecast is bound to become more optimistic and will more than likely be borne out by better putting on the course. But your positive thinking on the subject would have been merely wishful thinking if you had not put in the practice hours necessary to find a workable putting style and developed the confidence that grows from sinking a lot of practice putts. You can't will the ball into the hole, but having a strong self-concept about putting can allow you to make the best stroke you're capable of making.

A woman tour player once reflected on how she turned her game around and won again after a long slump on the ladies' pro tour: "I knew I just had to have more confidence in my game, because I could detect no mechanical problems.

"I had turned 40, and that's not the best thing in the world. At this time in life you're more susceptible to wondering about such things as, 'What have I been?' and 'What am I going to do?' I don't think young people would understand this at all, but everyone has hang-ups and self-doubts.

"Anyway, after giving it much thought, I decided if a person liked herself, then she'd do all right. Well, I just decided that I would like myself for what I did on the golf course, and go from there. . . ."

I decided I would like myself for what I did on the golf course. That is the best general definition we've found for a good golfing self-concept for players at any level.

19 THE POST-SHOT DEBRIEFING

What is the most obvious boost to a golfer's self-concept? *A good shot.*

What's the thing that hurts his self-concept the quickest? *A bad shot.*

What does that tell us? That the way in which we immediately process our good and bad shots in our minds can have a significant effect, for good or for bad, on our overall self-concept as golfers.

That is why a debriefing session should follow every shot you make during a round. A mere few seconds judiciously applied at this point can help you sustain the best possible realistic image of yourself as a golfer throughout the round.

One day club professional Davis Love saw a pupil of his, who was hitting last in her foursome, produce a terrific drive straight down the middle. Immediately, her foursome broke for the fairway.

Love ran over and blocked their path. "Stop!" he said. "Where are you running to so fast? I want you to *savor* that shot!"

Savoring a golf shot really means feeling it with the intuitive right hemisphere while it's still fresh—re-experiencing in your mind what your body just performed so rewardingly. It is not an ego trip or an exercise in self-adulation. Rather it is a practical method for engraving the good swing in your nerve and muscle system, so that it's easier to do again, and filing it in the feeling register that your INTEGRATOR maintains.

A short debriefing session after every shot provides an opportunity to mentally reinforce favorable swing results—and to neutralize unfavorable ones. It is also a process that leaves you psychologically fresh for your next shot.

So, when you do produce a good shot, stay with it for a few seconds. Savor it, enjoy it, feel it, re-experience it with your INTEGRATOR.

What about when you hit a *bad* shot?

Stay with the bad shot, too, but, again, only for

a few seconds, and this time only with your ANALYZER. Don't re-experience the effort. Evaluate it as a golf shot without becoming judgmental about the golfer.

Find out why the shot didn't come off as planned. Actually, you may have put your best swing on it, but used the wrong club for the yardage required or failed to take into account some non-swing factor such as wind conditions or the ball's lie. Your ANALYZER went to sleep. If you've made a bad shot with a good swing, there's really nothing to worry about—provided you rationally determine the non-swing cause of the failure. If you *don't* use your analytical powers, your right hemisphere may begin to produce anxiety feelings. Next time it has to produce a swing, the INTEGRATOR may be even more tentative, although it did nothing wrong the last time; it was your ANALYZER's fault the shot didn't come off. Thus, the INTEGRATOR won't respond to your swing cue quite so freely and this time may produce an outright bad swing.

Suppose you hit a bad shot because you did make a bad swing? Identify the error. Make a quick correction, rehearsing the positive move that would eliminate the error, then turn off both your left *and* right hemispheres as soon as you can. Find some totally unrelated diversion in nature to focus on, or strike up a conversation about something innocuous with one of your playing partners. Laugh it off or groan it off. Put your golf mind on a shelf until it's time to go into your setup routine for the next shot.

Or, think about one of the good shots you hit earlier. You can't forget the bad shot, but you can make the good shot or a lucky putt run interference and so keep the bad shot off your mind.

Re-experiencing the bad swing is unwise because it makes it easier to repeat the bad swing in the future. And over-analyzing a bad shot that is the result of a bad swing is masochistic. You caused it, but why get down on yourself and risk a string of mental errors?

The time to confront swing problems is when

your bad swings outnumber the good swings. And the place to confront them is on the practice tee, not on the golf course.

During the round, think of yourself as a member of some jury. Observe and weigh the evidence in each post-shot debriefing session. But don't pronounce yourself "guilty" of anything until you've finished playing. After the round is over, all the evidence is in, so you can pass "judgment" on your play without adversely affecting it and, like a judge, sentence yourself, if need be, to hard labor on the practice tee and no martinis for a month.

20 HOW TO BE YOUR OWN BEST COACH

When good teaching pros give clinics, they frequently find themselves making shots that they know they can't normally make during an actual playing round. If they're demonstrating wood play, they'll start fading and drawing their drives on command so well they'll wonder why they're not on tour. If they're demonstrating bunker play, they'll hole out tricky sand shots. If they're showing aspects of the short game, they'll hit the flagstick on chips and run putts in from improbable distances.

The power of positive suggestion accounts for this phenomenon, which coaches and instructors in many sports, not just in golf, experience.

The teachers talk as they demonstrate, and in trying to create a clear and coherent communication channel between teacher and pupil about the subject, they simultaneously create the ideal ANALYZER/INTEGRATOR relationship within their own minds.

One of us had a chance to play with the legendary former Oklahoma State golf coach, Labron Harris Sr. and, knowing his reputation as a putter, we looked forward to picking up a few tricks on the greens. Well into the round we decided there was nothing special about his technique. Finally, we realized it was his attitude, not his method, that let him sink so many putts. His faith in himself on the greens was total. He said he was a great putter, he believed it. And he was.

Harris used to make the players on his teams putt thousands of balls in a wooden track laid out on the practice green. This repetitious action not only grooved the collegians' putting strokes, but it showed them so many putts dropping into the cup (there was little chance for the ball to leave the track) that it helped their confidence, too.

Harris believed in practice partly because it built the good stroke, as he himself had learned, partly because it built a more favorable self concept.

He insisted on positive talking as well as positive thinking. If he heard one of his players say "three-putt" or "shank," he'd chase them off the course or out of the room.

According to educational psychologists, the trouble with negative language in teaching—"That's a mistake," "This is wrong," "Don't do that,"—is that it does not automatically foster the behavior you do want, and sometimes promotes just the opposite.

Tell a young child, "Don't say anything about how fat Aunt Tillie is" on your way to a family gathering and the first thing the child will ask her is, "How much do you weigh?"

But tell the child to ask Aunt Tillie about her cats or her job, and the child won't even notice Aunt Tillie's weight problem. By charting a specific course for the child to follow, the unwanted activity never comes up.

The analogy has been overused, but in certain ways the human mind really does function like a computer. Just as a computer is programmed to understand and respond to key words, so we light up at the sound of some words and not others. We may tell ourselves, "Don't slice" but the manner in which the mind receives that data is: *"Don't SLICE."* "Don't" is a weak, negative helping verb. "Slice" is a powerful, image-provoking action word.

The thousands of "don'ts" that comprise low-level golf instruction can be ineffectual and often destructive.

Swaying is a commonly heard diagnosis of a mis-hit among high-handicappers. But if you tell yourself, "Don't sway!" you may stand so rooted to the ground that you lose all weight transfer in your swing.

If, however, you say, "Brace that right knee!" you may eliminate the sway without interfering with the rhythm of the swing.

The ANALYZER is good at pinpointing the things that go wrong in our golf game and announcing them to us, but it requires a lot of work for it to be *constructively* analytical—to figure out a corrective measure for the situation.

Negative instruction doesn't always have "no's" or "don'ts" in it. For example, "Keep your head still!" can be a form of negative instruction in the sense that it does not necessarily promote *golf-appropriate* behavior. Almost all good golfers move their heads when they swing. Following the advice to keep your head rock-steady could result in a stiff, inhibited swing.

A more positive way of encouraging golf-appropriate behavior in this instance might be: "Keep yourself centered over the ball!" or "Swing around your center!" These phrases would allow for rotation, even of the head, around a center and so would free up the swing.

How do you address yourself during your various internal dialogues on the course? Do you use names like these?

bum	blockhead
donkey	dummy
idiot	jerk
turkey	klutz
ignoramus	stupid
hacker	dimwit

If we added the obscenities, the list could run for pages. The point is, such names automatically tarnish the self concept, whereas your own name, affectionately intoned, does not. Nor do these:

Arnie	buddy
partner	guy
pal	amigo
tiger	sweetheart
pro	baby
big fellow	Jack

A study of gymnasts preparing for the Olympics showed clearly that the most successful performers were the ones who talked to themselves constantly and always in favorable, positive terms.

Golfers can get into the habit of coaching themselves in the same way, on the practice tee and out on the course. Indeed, if you don't, who else will?

To illustrate the effect of the dialogue inside our heads upon behavior, consider two shots, a year apart, early in the career of Curtis Strange, a former All-American now on tour.

Year One, on the final hole of the NCAA Championship, Strange hit a superb 1-iron approach that stopped seven feet from the cup, setting up an eagle that gave him and his Wake Forest team the NCAA title.

Year Two, on the final hole of the arduous PGA Qualifying School Tournament, Strange pull-hooked a 6-iron into a bunker, then bogeyed to miss qualifying by one shot.

Two high-pressure spots to be in. Strange rose to the occasion in one case, blew it in the other. What accounts for the difference? This is how he recalls talking to himself as he stood up to make each shot:

As he addressed that 1-iron shot in the NCAA event, he thought, "Hit the best possible shot for the team!"

As he addressed the crucial 6-iron shot in the PGA Qualifier, he thought, "Don't miss this shot— if you do it'll cost money, and it'll cost six months off the tour!"

Year One: "best possible" and "for the team"—positive words filled with hope and optimism.

Year Two: "don't miss" and "it'll cost you"— negative words laden with threat, fear, near panic.

We can't always get good results by talking to ourselves positively. If there are mechanical flaws in our swing, no amount of sweet talk is going to help.

All we're saying is that the extent to which we can slant our internal dialogues on the golf course favorably and optimistically—as Curtis Strange did prior to hitting that winning shot in the NCAA (and apparently as he did again later in leading the pack in his second PGA Qualifier)— the better are our chances of playing our best possible shots.

Talking to yourself negatively is in some cases the articulation of the negative expectations we mentioned earlier, which pave the way for unwanted results. But golfers with high expectations also make the mistake of choosing negative language to urge themselves on, not realizing the language itself can cause their downfall.

Tell yourself, "Play to the center of the green!" rather than, "Stay out of that bunker on the left!" and you'll be less likely to pull the shot into the sand.

Tell yourself, "Let's see if we can par this hole," rather than, "Let's not get another double-bogey," and you'll improve your chances of ending up with a par or birdie.

Say, "Let's get the ball up to the hole," rather than, "Don't leave it short, stupid," and you're more likely to sink the putt.

If you're a 90 shooter, you're not going to break 80 just by coaching yourself through your next round of golf with positive language. But you won't soar to 100, either. And if you really get a strongly positive internal dialogue going whenever you do play, you are bound to pick up a few strokes—the strokes you have traditionally lost to the "can't-do" voice inside you.

21 LEAKS IN THE UMBRELLA

The way in which we talk to ourselves as golfers may be the single most important determinant of our self-concept during practice or play.

But there are some other potential stumbling blocks to a positive self-concept that you should be aware of.

Some of them, like the bad habit of always playing with golfers far superior in ability, can be controlled in a way to help your self-concept—and, therefore, your game—almost immediately.

Others, such as a miserable introduction to learning the game, or losing distance off the tee as you get older, take more effort to do something about. We believe in these instances that simply being aware of such things can help to alleviate the negative effects they may have on your self-concept.

In terms of our "umbrella," these are *leaks.* If we know what they are and where they are, we can duck them if nothing else. But in many cases, we can also plug and patch them with specific changes in behavior.

First experiences

We know a cocky young college golfer who's terrific at head-to-head match play, especially when the stakes are high or there are bad wind or weather conditions adding extra pressure to competition.

When we asked him where he got all his confidence, he thought a bit, then said it stemmed from an incident that occurred when he was playing in a basketball game for his seventh grade class. On this particular day, the opposing team fouled him on two consecutive plays toward the end of a close game, and he managed to make all four free throws. Ever since then, he told us, he's loved performing when the chips are down.

Obviously, we can't invent favorable early experiences in our athletic careers to foster such self-assurance (or, if we had *missed* all those shots, we couldn't easily forget the unfavorable experience), but we should take into account the influence that a first experience may have had on our present attitude. We *can* focus on the successes we have had. Even if the examples lack high drama, or come out not even approaching the number of failures, focusing on them can still subtly bolster our confidence and self-esteem.

We've all seen the fellow who takes his girlfriend, or the father his child, out for a lesson at the local driving range and in short order has the pupil whiffing balls in desperation. If the pupil is coerced into playing a round of golf while trying to absorb all that the well-meaning amateur teacher thinks he knows about technique, so much the worse. If it's on a weekend or holiday—as these sessions usually are—it will be like being sent into the combat zone with guns that you don't know how to fire. The pupil not only puzzles over all the intricacies of play, he worries about delaying or antagonizing the other golfers on the course.

Compare this slam-bang traumatic initiation to golf with the smooth head start Bobby Jones got under Stewart Maiden or Arnold Palmer under his father Deacon and you can appreciate how vastly different self-concepts in golf emerge.

Getting older

There's no denying the negative effect that aging can have on a golfer's self-concept. If, in a few short seasons in your 40's or 50's, you go from a 7 to a 15 handicap, you are certain to lose some of your passion for the game.

A few years ago, one of us had a chance to play with Paul Runyan, when he was 65. The former two-time PGA champion didn't think he was playing well at all. His drives were in the 200-210-yard range that day and he shot somewhere in the 80's. This type of performance clearly was affecting his self-concept.

But three years later, when we played with him

again, at age 68, Runyan had added 20-30 yards to his drives and this time he carded a 74. We asked him what accounted for the improvement. He said: "I got so disgusted with my game that I started doing exercises to get my strength and flexibility back." Runyan shot an opening-round 75 in the next PGA Championship on a very difficult course.

The single most pervasive source of a poor self-concept among older golfers is the loss of distance caused by the increasing restrictiveness and inflexibility of the muscular-skeletal system. Switching to lighter clubs and different shafts and playing from farther up on the tees may be good ways to cut those losses. But the most effective way is the route Paul Runyan took. You don't stop exercising because you get old. You get old because you stop exercising.

The battle against aging is in part a mental one. If you've been a good player up to a certain age, it suggests there is little wrong with your basic technique. If you start thinking you're over the hill, and now must experiment with your technique to get back that 10 yards per shot you're losing off the tee, you may well deal your swing mechanics a fatal blow.

A similar problem sometimes afflicts touring pros who have had to stop playing for a long time because of illness. If after recuperating from their illness or operation they return to competition too quickly, they discover their shots do things they have never seen before. That's because their hands are weaker, their muscles are out of condition, and their flexibility is poor. So they start changing things in their swing to compensate for these problems and, frequently, never again recover their winning technique.

As a player growing older, resolve to spend more time keeping yourself fit and resist making unnecessary changes in a technique that has carried you well thus far in the game. You'll find you'll keep your own technique effective longer and keep your scores low enough to sustain your interest and enjoyment.

Gender jinxes

There are some hang-ups that seem to be special to each sex that are worth noting because they are definitely related to self-concept and often can interfere with a player's progress in the game.

The big hang-up for men is distance. In fact, the philosophy of "How far?" has destroyed more talented young male players than any other single factor in the game. Women have never been obsessed with distance, but for most men, Golf's Golden Steps are those few yards you walk past your opponent's drive.

One way to break the stronghold that length may have on your mind—should you recognize that in yourself—is to play some rounds from the tee with the club you are *positive* will keep the ball in play. It might be a 4-wood or 5-iron, or it might be your driver—but it certainly won't be your driver on every par 4 and par 5 that you play. If you plan your day's tee shots in this manner, you'll be pleasantly surprised to find how controlling the ball helps control your score.

A lot of men also resist receiving instruction from others, a syndrome derived from the notion that it isn't "macho" to do so. They think, "If I can't figure out this game for myself, forget it!" Some men actively seek help—players such as Gary Player or Tommy Aaron are famous for listening to tips even from perfect strangers in the gallery. But they are in a minority. Women outnumber men on the lesson tee at least three to one because the men have had a hard time admitting they need help. And many of those men who are willing to submit to a lesson actually go out on the practice tee not to receive advice, but to tell the pro how to do it.

The typical male attitude toward instruction is undergoing some change today, however. Certainly all the men who could use help have not yet signed up for lessons from their pros, but more of them appear to regard outside instruction as a feasible and relatively shameless path toward improvement. Maybe this is because they've lost so many

Nassaus they're desperate. Most likely, the increased sophistication of instructors and their programs and the greater respect given the how-to-be-better philosophy generally, in today's society, account for the change.

Unlike men, who frequently have a high fear of failure, women have had a high fear of success, especially in traditionally male endeavors, which nearly all sports have been. In the early days of women's professional golf, many of the tour players genuinely worried about whether winning an event would cost them friends on the circuit.

Although Billie Jean King trounced Bobby Riggs several years ago in tennis, for some women the fear or anxiety about competition apparently is still a problem. One survey of female medical school students, for example, showed that although the women greatly relished training to become doctors, they had mixed feelings about actually completing their studies at graduation time.

On Ladies' Day, you'll often find that most of the women are in the clubhouse sipping coffee — and they stay there right up until tee-off time. The individual who does practice and otherwise compete seriously may be subtly ostracized by the others for playing "too aggressively" or for being "out to win."

On Men's Day, by contrast, there are dozens of players tuning up on the putting green, or hitting balls off the practice tee, before the matches start.

But some change has been brought about by the feminist movement. Congress has passed Title IX, the law which guarantees equal sports facilities and programs for men and women in any federally funded secondary school or college. In the past few years, we have observed that young college women not only find it respectable to compete in many different sports, including golf, but find it enjoyable and don't worry as much about being typecast as "jocks." It's our guess that because of this, there'll be a lot more traffic on the practice tee on Ladies' Days in the future.

Lack of equitable competition

Your self-concept is strongly influenced by the company you keep. We have a friend who is a six-footer, but he spent his four college years living in a basketball dorm where the sinks and mirrors and other fixtures were all raised an extra six inches to a foot for the benefit of the extremely tall players. By the time he graduated, our friend thought he was one of the shorter men on campus.

Playing with golfers who are much better than you is a great experience — every so often. But constant competition with golfers who are 10 shots or more per round better than you is bound to hurt your idea of yourself as a golfer. Participants in many other sports don't really have this problem. Ability automatically seeks its own level in tennis, for example. Golf's handicapping system permits fair competition between players of vastly different skills. You're not being fair to yourself psychologically, however, if you're always the one with the highest handicap in your favorite foursome.

In trying to build up your golfing self-concept, bear in mind that good shotmaking is somewhat relative. We watched George Archer trying out a variety of new graphite drivers one day. Most golfers would trade their IBM stock for any one of the towering 280-yard drives he produced with the clubs. But Archer wasn't happy: "They went too straight," he told us later. "I was trying to work the ball and I couldn't."

Another time we saw Sam Snead experimenting with a new sand wedge. After hitting a bucket of balls all to within four to six feet of the pin, he gave the club back to the company rep standing nearby and said, "Naw. I want my shots to flutter more and land like a butterfly."

Anyway, if you're in the company of players who are far superior to you, you really could play the round of your life and no one would notice. Consistently failing to get recognition for extra good efforts is a bummer.

We're not suggesting that you arrange to play

all your golf with a personal fan club or mutual admiration society. But do recognize the favorable effect on your self-concept that genial and reasonably supportive playing partners can have.

This particular fact was borne out in a study conducted some time ago on a group of young men who bowled together every week. It was determined that one of the fellows could score as well as, if not higher than, all his friends when he bowled on his own. But in the group, he always scored near the bottom, because his self-concept couldn't handle the jeers and taunts that were an accepted part of the social routine.

Biting off more than you can shoot

Set unrealistic goals for yourself and you automatically set a trap for your self-concept.

We know a highly successful radiologist who thinks he ought to be shooting in the low 70's because he's been playing the game for two years. He expects so much of himself that if he mis-hits his first few shots, he will pack it in. He plays more three-hole rounds than anybody we know.

The same problem results if you club yourself according to your career-high yardage with each club rather than your average yardage. Going for your best-ever shot every time simply puts too much pressure on the swing. It extends a carte-blanche invitation to mis-hits and leaves too many shots short even when the swing does hold up.

Taming nothing but monsters

Playing all your golf on 7,000-yard-long courses is another way of biting off more than you can shoot. Psychologically, it can foster a grim self-concept.

Playing nothing but short patsy courses is not much of an answer, either.

For most golfers, the solution lies somewhere in between. Tackle the challenging layout when you can find it — but don't turn your back on the more ordinary course which in fact offers you a better

chance for putting a couple of creditable perform-
ances on the scorecard, thus enhancing your self-
worth.

One successful collegiate coach, whose team
has an extremely tough home course, won't let his
golfers play from the championship markers more
than two rounds a week because he doesn't want
them to get used to coming in with nothing but
high numbers. If they play from the regular tees a
couple of times, they experience lower scores,
which may stand them in good stead when they are
scoring well in actual competition.

Scoring barriers

There are performance barriers in golf that are
based on realistic things such as physical skill and
strength, and there are other barriers that are in
part a function of our self-concept.

At the highest level, playing a round under 60
was, until recently when Al Geiberger achieved it, a
kind of scoring barrier that had become almost as
much a mental barrier as a physical one. Like the
four-minute mile in running, though, maybe the
under-60 round will become more common now.

Golfers get used to scoring in a certain range
and this sometimes keeps them from achieving
greater success when it is within their reach. If you
shoot in the 95-100 range normally, that is your
comfortable scoring range. If you reach the 16th
hole needing only consecutive bogeys to break 90, a
"this isn't me" attitude may take over and cause you
to give the course back a half-dozen shots so that
you finish inside your familiar scoring range.

What prevents you from going beyond your
usual limits is something akin to the negative self-
fulfilling prophecy. Only in this case, you are not
embracing a mediocre performance so much as you
are withdrawing from a potentially fine one out of
discomfort with the unknown.

If, for example, you find yourself on the green in
two on a par 5 you usually bogey, and if the thought
suddenly crosses your mind that you shouldn't be

playing this hole this well, you will very likely find a way to three- or maybe four-putt.

If you normally shoot in the low 90's but toward the end of one particularly good round you discover you are within striking distance of your first 88 or 89, beware of thinking in the future tense or you may well mis-hit enough shots to come in with another 93.

Psychologist Peter Cranford draws the analogy that a good round of golf is a string of pearls. Each good shot is a precious pearl that takes your full attention to create. You can only create one at a time, so don't concern yourself with those you've made already or those you have yet to make. Focusing on adding one pearl, individually, leads to the creation of a fine finished product.

If a player gets ahead in a tournament and has never been there before, the first thing he's got to fight is the question: "What am I doing here?" It happens frequently in high-level competition — that's why so many first-round front-runners in major events like the U.S. Open are seldom heard from later in the week.

But there are two ways to process the information of failing to fulfill the promise of an early lead or breaking a scoring barrier that was in your reach. One is negative: to see in what happened the confirmation of the belief that you belong where you are now. The other is positive: to read into what happened proof that you can break that barrier (since you came so close) and to wait for your next chance. The more often you come near your particular barrier, the more comfortable you will feel, psychologically, and eventually it will not seem that strange to be doing so well.

Early in his career, Tom Watson was unjustly regarded by some as a choker because he came so close to winning major tournaments, only to lose them through poor play in the final round. But Watson never made that label part of his self-concept. And the more often he experienced being in or near the lead in a big tournament, the lower the barrier got.

22 CHARGE THE COURSE OR SEDUCE IT?

Consider these few questions briefly, then check the answers that suit you best:

1. On days when my short-iron shots are biting and holding the green especially well, it is most often because:
   a) I'm striking the ball crisply by hitting down and through it rather than scooping it. ☐
   b) The greens are unusually damp and soft, so everyone's shots are holding well. ☐

2. When I win in match play against a tough opponent, it is usually because:
   a) I am able to get myself up for this type of match and I concentrate well against tough competition. ☐
   b) My opponent has an off day and doesn't play up to his/her capabilities. ☐

3. On days when I just can't get it together and nothing seems to go right for me on the course, I can usually trace the causes to:
   a) My lack of preparation for playing on these days and, hence, my poor concentration. ☐
   b) Outside factors such as job tensions, noisy caddies, inconsiderate playing partners, etc. ☐

4. Most of my poor shots from sand traps can usually be traced to:
   a) My inability to remember and apply the basic principles for a good sand shot. ☐
   b) Inconsistent sand texture from hole to hole on the courses I play

(i.e., on some holes the sand is thick and fluffy while on other holes the sand is sparse but packed down hard to the earth). □

5. On those occasions when I've been able to get my game back after suffering three or four disastrous holes and turn my game around by playing the remaining holes particularly well, it is most often because:

   a) I was able to control my emotions and not yield to the temptation to give up and merely play the round out. □

   b) I got a lucky break or two on a hole and this caused me to regain my composure. □

Our outlook toward the golf course is shaped partly by how much control we feel we have over the things around us. This attribute of our self-concept can significantly help or hurt us.

If you answered most of the questions above by checking the "a" boxes, you are probably a person who feels you exert *personal control* over your environment.

If you answered the questions by checking the "b" responses, chances are you feel that what you do is largely controlled by *outside* factors. (A truly valid test to determine these characteristics would involve many more items similar to those given above.)

The question as to whether a person is *in charge* of his environment, or *in the hands* of it, becomes a problem in golf if one has an exaggerated notion either way.

Let's take an extreme example of the take-charge attitude. A person with this comes straight out of the mainstream of American business society—and without him (or her) there might not be 500 solvent companies on the Fortune 500 list.

As board chairman, or department head, or sales manager, or editor-in-chief, this person *has* to believe not only that he knows what's going on, but that he is responsible for it happening.

Total belief in personal sovereignty and power is a problem on the golf course because the vagaries and vicissitudes of the game challenge that belief at regular intervals. If you really think you're master out there just as you are in the board room, then bad lies, or shots that don't come off as planned, are much more likely to threaten, upset, disappoint or anger you.

Total belief in the power of *outside* factors to control your life also leads to problems on the golf course. Many studies have been done to compare how people perform on tests when they're told skill is involved, on one hand, or luck, on the other. Invariably, the people who think skill is involved put more effort into their responses than those who think it's all luck and so score better. If they think it's luck, they shrug their shoulders and tend to ignore the experience they gain in actually doing the test.

In golf, the same syndrome crops up when the extreme outside-control believer arrives in Florida from New York for a golf vacation and refuses to adapt his putting game to the exigencies of Bermuda greens. He's used to bent-grass greens where you get what you see, and rather than read into the new greens the extra break required by the grain, he just resigns himself to not being able to putt for the week.

The personality most effective in golf has to have a bit of both control attitudes in it.

When you do feel you're the boss, you put more time and effort into practice and so you really begin to master the game. If this represents a *realistic* sense of control over your environment, you won't be destroyed when things outside your power come along.

Young pros on tour often falter on pressure shots because they're trying to exert too much personal control. Mental over-control results in physical over-control, which keeps them from swinging their best. Similarly in baseball, an inexperienced pitcher will be inclined to point his pitch, almost as though he were tossing darts, rather than throw it, on a 3-2 count, and chances are he'll put the ball in the dirt or up in the backstop.

A mentally mature golfer may use expressions such as "Let it hap'n, Cap'n," "Aim and hang loose," or "Let 'er fly," in pressure situations. In effect, he's urging himself to make that leap from ANALYZER to INTEGRATOR that he usually makes under normal pressure. He's done all that is humanly possible. He knows he can't control the shot once it starts, but that he can ruin it before it starts if he doesn't relax.

Another golfer might focus on experiencing lighter grip pressure in tight spots to help him get an arms-hanging feeling and prevent over-control.

Note that "Let it happen" is not the same as "Make it happen," which suggests too much control, or "Let's see what happens," which suggests too little. There's got to be a blend of attitudes.

The idea of "charging the course" as Arnold Palmer did so often in winning tournaments in the 1950's and 60's romanticized the concept of personal control in golf and encouraged more people to go on the attack than really had the ability or determination to do so.

Maybe if you have so much drive that by now you also have your own Lear Jet, you can force your way into the teeth of every hard hole that comes along.

We think players are much more likely to benefit from an attitude like Hale Irwin's which sees the golf course more as an environment to be "seduced," than to be charged or attacked. Irwin certainly is not giving up personal control in his own game. Far from it. (Interestingly, when Irwin wins a tournament, it is almost always on a "tough" course.) But he's playing the course as he finds it—taking his birdies where he can but settling for pars where he has to, keeping his drives in the fairways and playing for the centers of the greens. If a par 5 is so hard to play with a driver and a 3-wood that he'll make either 4 or 7, then Irwin's willing to concede that one to the environment (unless a special tournament situation exists) and play two 2-irons and a wedge.

The zone defense in modern pro football has forced quarterbacks to pass to the seams and the sidelines, patiently taking what short gains the zone allows them. In the same way, tough golf holes, or rough weather conditions, force golfers to adjust games and expectations to what the layout offers, rather than "throwing the bomb" on every shot.

If anyone thinks this form of seduction isn't effective or exciting, he never saw a Johnny Unitas or Ken Stabler take a team downfield with a couple of minutes to go or watched Jack Nicklaus patiently stalk a links course in the British Open.

Trying to cut the corner on a dangerous dogleg in order to hit your next shot with an iron one or two numbers smaller is an example of throwing the bomb unnecessarily. Keeping your drive in the middle is the safe shot—taking what the course gives you.

Swinging from the heels on your second shot in order to carry the water to a par 5 is an example of throwing the bomb unnecessarily. Laying up and then making the short pitch is the strategy that the Irwin-type percentage golfer would normally use.

23 "OUR DEEPEST SYMPATHY"

A friend of ours passes out the "sympathy card" reprinted below whenever one of his cronies gets carried away describing his misfortunes on the golf course.

Storytelling or fable-building is one of three fairly common types of egocentric, self-conscious behavior among golfers. These egocentricities have more to do with the *maturity* of personality than with personality *per se*, for they trap us into thinking and acting like adolescents. They cost strokes because they draw your attention away from the shot at hand, or produce unrealistic assessments about what's going on around you.

✝ *Our Deepest Sympathy*

We're sorry for your trouble.   Never in the long and chequered history of this club has any golfer suffered such a calamitous sequence of ill luck as you have. Our hearts bleed for you and will you please accept this small token of our deepest sympathy.

Egocentric hazard 1: "They're watching me."

This is the most common and perhaps the most easily recognizable of the three forms of egocentricity that can waste strokes in golf.

Psychologists call it the "imaginary-audience" syndrome and it's what drives teenagers to spend so much time standing in front of a mirror thinking about their appearances. They are convinced everyone is always looking at them under a microscope. But the microscope is in their own heads.

Club golfers are most likely to succumb to the imaginary syndrome when:

—driving off a crowded first tee;

—playing through a slow group on the course;

—hitting to a par 3 after they've been waved on by the preceding group;

—playing with someone who may be a much better golfer than they are, such as the club pro or the local amateur whiz.

Better golfers are not necessarily immune to the problem. It will crop up in the young touring pro, for example, the first time he tees off in the Masters or in any tournament when he gets to the holes carried on national television.

In any of these situations, if you are thinking about what other people may be thinking as they watch you, you're much more likely to become over-cautious in your setup or alignment, trying to do everything right, or you may rush to get the shot over with and get out of there. Your left hemisphere is so active your right hemisphere never gets in the act.

It really doesn't matter if you react to the imaginary audience as a showboat ("I'm going to show them how far I can hit the ball!") or with stage fright ("Please, God, don't let me put it in the lake in front of all these people!").

Either way, the shot will suffer because your mind is attending to it in too self-conscious a way. Both ANALYZER and INTEGRATOR are being mis-used.

The irony is that the audience you think you have may not really be there in these situations. You may think all eyes are on you when you're teeing it up on the first hole but, in fact, your playing partners may be fiddling with their gloves or studying the cloud formations.

You may think the club pro is staring critically at your forward press when he joins your foursome for a hole or two, when, in fact, his mind is on whether he has enough carts for the member-guest coming up.

You may think the players in the preceding foursome, standing off to the side as your group hits onto a par-3 green, are sizing up your skill with a 7-iron, when they're actually worried about their own putts coming up and don't really care if you hit it into the cup or into the woods.

There is no denying the intensity of the self-consciousness that accompanies the imaginary-audience syndrome. Specifically, we know a fine woman golfer who, years ago as the top young amateur in her area, found herself paired with the defending U.S. Open champion in the opening round of that event which was being played at her home club. On the first tee, the girl was so over-whelmed with thoughts about what the touring pro might think of her swing and what her hometown gallery may have expected of her, that she actually felt her knees knocking.

She topped her drive; but what proved the depth of feeling involved in that experience was the fact that the poor girl was plagued by a recurring dream about it for years afterward. In the dream, as she related it, before a large gallery on the opening hole she would try and try, but repeatedly fail to make contact with the ball. Finally, Joseph C. Dey Jr., a father figure in the world of amateur golf, would step from the crowd and yank her off the tee with a giant hook.

Antidote: Play your own game

One way to avoid the imaginary-audience syndrome is to take pains to adhere to your normal pre-shot routine or to focus on one aspect of it, such as your alignment, with particular attentiveness. The idea is to get your ANALYZER so thoroughly involved that the onlookers will "vanish." This is the style that Ben Hogan epitomized. His ANALYZER was so involved in his game that potential outside distractions did not exist for him.

Egocentric Hazard 2: "Once upon a time. . . ."

The adolescent is constantly making up stories about himself as a necessary part of his quest for identity. By tinkering with reality here and there, he is able to experiment with different roles, feelings and thoughts, seeing himself sometimes as hero, sometimes as victim and eventually, we hope, figuring out the things about himself that are solid and true.

The immature golfing personality also slips into fantasizing. He makes up fables about what happens to himself on the course as a way of avoiding the fact that his game has limitations and defects.

Some of the pros who have to play the Monday morning qualifier on tour become particularly inventive about their rounds whenever they fail to win a spot in the tournament that week. For a few rabbits, missing on Monday by one stroke, particularly after missing by a close margin several times in a row, becomes almost as valuable to them, in the form of material for a "you-won't-believe-this-one" story, as actually making it. You can overhear accounts like this one in the grill:

"I was needing only a double on the last hole to get in. It's a short par 4 with an O.B. right, so I go for a safety with a 2-iron off the tee. I flush it in the center and walk out to find my ball in a bad divot hole. The track is a dog, all chopped up, and they're playing it down. I get nervous over my 8-iron, pull it to the left and it catches a bunker. Well, you know how it's rained with the washouts? Well, the sand's gone where my ball is. I hit a firm spot, blade it over the green to guess where? O.B. Make 7 and miss by one! Why me?"

A bad shot might lead to this sort of speculative musing: "Gee, I wouldn't have to make this putt to stay even if I hadn't bounced into the trap on 14."

A good shot might stimulate this fantasy: "Hey, I'm in good position to make par here. Now, if I can just get a bogey on that long par 4 coming up, and then birdie 16, and make two pars going in, I'll break 90 for the first time this year! Wait'll I tell them in the clubhouse!"

Note that one fable draws the golfer into the past and the other into the future. The only shot that counts—the one coming up—isn't on his mind at all, and that's the problem.

Antidote: Stay in the "present tense."

On specific shots, a good way to keep your mind from wandering into fable-building is to talk to yourself in the present tense and not use the words "if only."

"All right, I'm playing my favorite club, a fairway wood, grip's okay, I've got a good lie, now get your grip, good setup, feels right, let her fly. . . ." This sort of friendly inner voice may keep you locked in the present.

Fable-building is as much a drain on the average golfer's energy and concentration as is the imaginary-audience syndrome. It can be a bigger problem simply because there's so much free time in golf to mis-use it this way—and so much raw material to work from.

Either you concoct fables out of things around you, like the weather, course conditions or other golfers, or you base them on your own shots.

If you draw on outside factors, you tell yourself things like, "Every time I go to hit a shot the wind is blowing!" or, "How am I supposed to putt on these bumpy greens?" You ignore the fact that your fellow golfers also have the wind and bumpy greens to contend with. Under proper direction, your scenario becomes so real to you that you find more and more evidence to support the tragic theme as you go along, and by the time you get into the clubhouse you're ready for Hollywood.

It's easy to base fables on your own shots because they're so important to you, and also because each one remains fresh in your mind for so long after you hit it.

Egocentric Hazard 3: "If he can do it, so can I"

Youngsters are quick to jump to false assumptions about a lot of things and slow to admit their errors even when the evidence stares them in the face. Two things happen together in time, or are connected in some other way, and the youngster assumes they are related as cause and effect. Psychologists call this form of thinking an "assumptive reality," and it affects golfers as well as teenagers.

An assumptive reality that a lot of the newcomers to the pro tour have to conquer is one that relates distance off the tee with effectiveness in tournament competition at the highest level. The young pros hit for maximum distance as if to prove they're worthy of the TPD card they've just won. Most of them wean themselves of this illusion after discovering they are consistently coming off the course with higher numbers than players who are 20 or 30 yards shorter with the driver.

Distance is integral to most of the assumptive realities afflicting club golfers, too. We once played in a foursome that included a rugged football tackle and a skinny scratch amateur player. At the start, the football player jumped to the conclusion that since he outweighed the good golfer by 100 pounds, he ought to take two clubs less than he on every shot of equal length that they faced. We discreetly kept track of what this false assumption cost the football player during the round—at least 12 shots and two lost balls.

Many golfers not only commonly club themselves according to the longest hitter in the foursome they're playing in, but also according to the longest shot they've ever produced with a particular club. If a fellow's career 7-iron went 155 yards, then that becomes his basis for hitting all 7-irons. Result? He leaves most of his 7-iron shots short or, by overswinging in order to achieve that best-ever length, he mis-hits them completely.

Superstitious behavior is a form of assumptive reality not necessarily harmful in golf. If wearing an all-black outfit puts Gary Player in a winning frame of mind, or avoiding the use of No. 3 balls keeps Sandra Palmer from worrying about three-putting, we can hardly disapprove. Neither action contributes directly to better performance, but both may pave the way for better performance simply by easing the mind a bit. The problem for most golfers arises when they adopt non-functional mannerisms of the stars and expect miracles.

We know a club pro who sandpapered his fingertips to improve his putting touch for his state PGA after reading in the paper that pro football wide receiver Tommy McDonald had done the same thing to help him hold onto more passes. The golf pro related receiving in football with putting in golf and the next day his hands were so raw he had to withdraw from the tournament.

Antidote: Use your ANALYZER

Egocentric Hazard 3 is a more straightforward intellectual problem than the previous two; and mainly you need your ANALYZER to stay out of it. The problem of under-clubbing yourself, for example, is easily solved if you take the time some day to step off your distances with each club. Find your range from short to long with each club, and the medium zone that gives you control and distance with a comfortable effort. And copying what other golfers do isn't necessarily a bad thing. But have your ANALYZER check it out to make sure it has a chance to work for you.

24 WILL YOUR DOG BITE YOU IF YOU MISS THAT PUTT?

The last thing we want to say about the role of personality and attitudes in two-hemisphere golf is on perspective.

Cary Middlecoff used to negate the effects of a poor shot on himself during a tournament by musing, "Well, my wife still loves me and I have some money in the bank, and when I go home my dog won't bite me."

That's keeping things in perspective. There's nothing wrong with taking yourself seriously out on the golf course. But if you take yourself solemnly, you put too much pressure on yourself before each shot and give yourself too much grief and static when a shot doesn't come off as planned.

That's getting things out of perspective.

Everyone gets a turn at having a bad day on the golf course. The greatest golfers in history have had terrible rounds and managed to take them in stride. Francis Ouimet became the first American-born winner of the U.S. Open after firing a horrendous 87 in the practice round before the event.

Jack Nicklaus, possibly the classiest runner-up ever, in addition to being a gracious winner, missed the Grand Slam by a mere three shots in 1975, yet never lost his cool. "Really, it's just a game," he said to an associate shortly after losing the British Open.

Arnold Palmer patiently answered questions in the press tent for an hour after dismally failing to make the cut one year in the PGA, the only major title to have eluded him, on a course he knew and loved—Canterbury in Ohio. We recall the very first question he had to handle: "Arnold, are you disappointed?"

People maintain their perspective by using common sense, humor and some healthy rationalization. When former Mets' relief ace Tug McGraw would be called in to put out some late-inning rally, he'd keep calm and relaxed by telling himself as he walked out to the mound that in 30 million years the earth would be a frozen snowball, so why worry about a couple of men on base in Shea Stadium now?

A golfer we know jogs himself back to reality after making a bad shot by contemplating the existence of 800 million Chinese on the other side of the world who are going about their business totally oblivious to his troubles.

A sane and healthy perspective on the game actually helps performance. Joe Inman, after staying up half the night attending the birth of his son, flew to the West Coast and, on only a couple of hours' sleep, teed it up in the first round of the Tournament of Champions. Shooting a 69, he later accounted for his low score:

"I had just witnessed the birth of my son, and that makes you realize that some things are more important than birdies and bogeys. I love golf and I never give it less than my best, but I was relaxed that first day because I thought about my wife and child, and suddenly golf didn't seem like such a life-and-death matter."

Loss of perspective is related to the control problem discussed earlier. The extreme personal-control personality, in addition to trying to will his way around the golf course, tends to shoulder all the blame himself for his playing mistakes.

The extreme outside-control type, who feels the course is a kind of giant roulette wheel dictating his fortunes, tends to read into his bad shots a dooms-day message about his golfing lot generally.

If you blindly commit ego and emotion to doing well on the course, then you won't accept the in-evitability of error or be able to cope with bad luck, and you'll have an awful time out there. So will your playing partners, for no one enjoys the company of a moaner or a quitter.

Before every round he played, Walter Hagen reminded himself that he would make a half-dozen bad shots that day. And usually he would—but they did not take him by surprise when they came, so they didn't continue to bother him or hurt his ability to score.

When Bobby Locke mis-hit a shot during a round, he put it out of his mind at once by sizing up possibilities for the next shot. He was firmly opposed to "holding an inquest" after making a mistake because he believed it prolonged the agony unnecessarily and led to more mistakes.

Putting is the part of the game where self-confidence counts the most, and it is no accident that here more than anywhere else, good players should avoid becoming too critical about their failures. Touring pros routinely blame their caddies, their putters or lapses in concentration for missed putts. Or they get into the press tent and knock the greens, an unattractive, but quite functional, defense mechanism. Rarely do they pin the blame on their putting strokes, where it might be argued their "identity" truly resides.

There actually are sound reasons for rationalizing failure on the greens—and your ANALYZER should know them.

For one thing, even perfectly struck putts will miss the cup a lot of times because of flaws and inconsistencies in the putting surface. An engineer named David Pelz has done studies which prove this conclusively. Pelz built a miniature ski-slope device, the "True Roller," which allowed him to "putt" a ball from exactly the same distance in exactly the same fashion every time. Yet, he missed three out of 10 putts from 13 feet on excellent-quality greens, four out of 10 on good-quality greens and five out of 10 on poor-quality greens. That's with a perfect aim and a perfect stroke.

Also, as Gene Sarazen has observed, the older we get, the more experience works against us on the greens. Youngsters can putt the eyes out of a course because they don't have a backlog of failure to consult when they face a putt. Veterans simply have seen too many putts, well-struck putts as well as bad ones, miss the hole. As one told us, "I just know more ways to miss 'em than those kids."

In view of this special difficulty posed by the putting game, it is not really a contradiction to say that we must take responsibility for our putting strokes, but not necessarily for the putts we miss.

That has been the attitude of Nicklaus, one of the game's greatest putters. Once, teamed with Tom Weiskopf in an important Ryder Cup match, he had a 12-foot putt and Weiskopf an 8-foot putt on a certain green. Tom walked up intending to mark his ball, then go to school on Jack's putt since it was on the same line.

"Pick it up," said Nicklaus.

"What do you mean?" said Weiskopf.

"I've got this made."

"Are you crazy?" Weiskopf replied. "We're only 1 up."

"Don't worry, I've got the putt made."

Weiskopf marked his ball anyway—luckily, for Jack's putt veered wide of the cup at the last moment.

Weiskopf said, "Good thing I marked." Then Nicklaus made a remark that revealed the depth of his confidence in his putting:

"I made that putt," he said. "It just didn't happen to go in the hole."

Other pros view the whole business of putting as something controlled by Providence—another form of outside-control philosophy. Tommy Bolt was good at this. He'd look up at the heavens if he missed a short one and say "Why me?—and he'd look up whenever he snaked in a 40-footer, too.

Nothing really surprised Bolt on the greens. Once he was paired with Al Besselink in a tournament. Bolt was standing by on the green at the last hole when he saw Bessie bend over to mark his ball after a crucial lag putt. Besselink accidentally dropped his putter which was under his arm. The putter landed, hit Bessie's ball and the ball skittered into the cup.

Tommy didn't even blink.

PART IV
EMOTIONS

Dealing with deep emotions

The new golf mind consists of a two-hemisphere brain connected by a bridge and influenced by the "umbrella" that we say represents a golf-effective personality.

There is one last element in this model. We haven't mentioned it until now partly because at first glance it would seem to contain the sort of familiar material that comes up whenever people talk about "golf psychology."

We're talking about the mind's power source—the basic life energies and emotions that create distinctive human personalities and that drive people to try to excel in things like golf in the first place.

We need energy in the form of motivation simply to want to play golf. But to play golf well we must experience some emotional arousal. An under-aroused golfer has little or no traffic moving on the bridge between his hemispheres.

But we can't have too much energy, either. An over-aroused golfer can have a traffic jam on the bridge between hemispheres which could result in confusion, frustration or over-excitement and, ultimately, poor scores.

So let's look at the question of how much arousal is beneficial. Then we'll point out how energy in the wrong form hampers the right hemisphere's ability to execute the swing by flooding it with feelings. Fear, anger, joy, despair—any and all of these emotions can turn INTEGRATOR into DISINTEGRATOR.

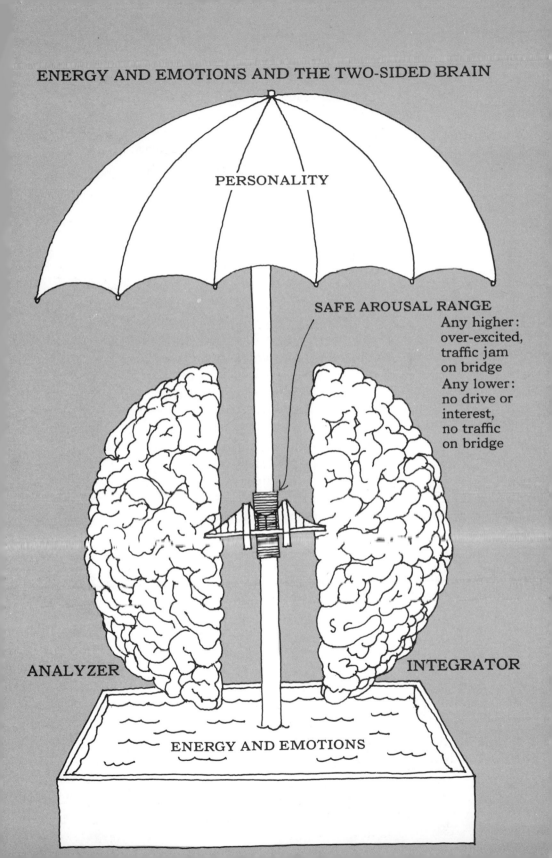

ENERGY AND EMOTIONS AND THE TWO-SIDED BRAIN

PERSONALITY

SAFE AROUSAL RANGE

Any higher:
over-excited,
traffic jam
on bridge

Any lower:
no drive or
interest,
no traffic
on bridge

ANALYZER

INTEGRATOR

ENERGY AND EMOTIONS

25 VARIETIES OF AROUSAL

Example A:
  "The first day of our member-member, I was determined to do well, but I got tense and couldn't do anything right. The next day, when our team was out of contention, I relaxed and shot 12 strokes better."

Example B:
  "I was on a special two-week vacation with a large group of golfers. I played and practiced nearly every day in expectation of a chance to win the tournament planned for the group for the last day. I really wanted to do well, but when the tournament was finally played, I found myself hitting some shots as though I didn't care what happened, and the results proved it—I finished 16th out of 24."

These scenarios show the bad effects of too much and too little arousal.

The golfer in Example A got himself so "up" for the opening round of his tournament that he evidently couldn't play his normal game. When his arousal level dropped into the functional range on the second day, he played much better.

The golfer in Example B had played so much more golf than his usual schedule of one or two rounds a week at home, that he became under-aroused—mentally and physically stale. He might have told himself, "This is important," but it didn't get him motivated. He was not conditioned to such intense golfing activity, of a kind that the tour player contends with regularly.

If Johnny Miller analyzed the cases, he would say both golfers had failed to keep an eye on their "emotional tachometers." Miller's theory on arousal: "I believe that within every golfer's brain is something similar to a car's tachometer, with a red line that shows your maximum safe level of emotion. The trick is to know when it is reaching the danger level, when you're getting too excited to play well, and then reduce it to a safe level."

Good football coaches recognize that even in their highly aggressive sport, too much arousal can be a bad thing and lead to costly fumbles and penalties. That's why they'll refrain from giving pep talks to players who are naturally "up" or before games that have so much tradition or significance that the whole team is geared up automatically.

The challenge in golf is to be physically aroused without becoming tense, to be mentally relaxed without becoming indifferent.

The tension that the body feels as a result of too much arousal leads directly to bad shots in two ways:

1) *It tightens and inhibits the swinging muscles.* Although you may not literally break into a sweat over a bad lie in a sand trap, for example, the tension produced by the challenge may cause you to tighten your muscles in the hitting area, thus shortening your swing arc width. This would raise the club just enough to make you skull the ball.

2) *It activates other muscles at an inappropriate time.* Hitting from the top with the right hand is a common example of this property of tension. The hands in particular tend to get overactive—just as they do in a heated conversation—and this throws your swing arc and your timing out of whack.

An optometrist named Bill Harrison has done studies showing that tension also can create blurred vision in golfers. You have your eye on the ball, but if you're fearful of missing a short putt you may not be able to focus on it properly, because your thoughts will be in the past (on a putt of the same length that you missed two holes ago) or in the future (on the possible consequences of your missing this putt). Changing from the present tense causes refocusing of the eyes and a temporary blur in vision.

Your pre-round and pre-shot routines can help you stay at your own proper arousal level. Recognize the situations that automatically generate tension, then be sure to adhere to your routines. By focusing on the things to do in your routine, you'll block out distractions or annoyances. You'll keep nice and relaxed. You'll stay cool.

Tournament play tends to over-arouse most club golfers, so the pre-round routine should be meticulously observed. If you don't normally buy new balls or a brand new shirt before playing golf, don't buy them on the day of a big match, or they'll add to the unique feelings you are already experiencing. Stick to the tried-and-true. Avoid novelty, unfamiliar things.

Trying to get extra distance breeds tension. In fact, several tour players who have made it to the finals of the National Long Driving Championship have admitted to feeling more nervous there than they ever felt teeing off in the Open. The mental tension gets to the muscles, which is why some wild, erratic shots are produced in these contests by normally consistent drivers.

Another interesting point about long-driving contests: it's hard to gear down to your normal driving game once you have revved up for a full effort. Good players usually try to steer clear of driving contests if they're scheduled prior to other important events, because the big-shot effort ruins their timing. That's also why any player hitting a lot of full drives before a round may not be doing his swing any favors. When you hit a few good ones on the range, there's a tendency to stretch for just a few more yards, and that effort carries you past your exertion range for peak performance and makes it hard for you to get back where you belong.

Important putts breed tension, too. In football

it is common for coaches to call time-out before crucial field goal attempts by the opposition to put extra pressure on the kicker. We know a coach who counteracts this tactic by getting together with his kicker and going over simple mechanics with him. The player doesn't need a lesson, but the ploy gets his mind off the results of his efforts coming up. The golfer faced with a crucial short putt does the same thing when he focuses on something simple like taking the club straight back and straight through, instead of worrying about missing.

Tough courses tend to over-arouse you. We have a friend who periodically plays a course where there are out-of-bounds areas on 17 of the 18 holes. He claims he can't relax and play properly until he knocks a ball O.B. After that the course doesn't bother him.

But every discussion we've ever heard concerning some great new monster course inevitably concludes that it is not that hard to score on "if you can keep it down the middle." The "monster" in most long layouts is really within the golfer's mind. If you use your ANALYZER sensibly, play percentage shots, especially off the tee, and let the INTEGRATOR do its thing, you'll be surprised how undaunted you can be playing these top courses.

Simple relaxation techniques can keep you from getting over-aroused, too. If you feel yourself tensing up on your way to an important shot, hold your club between thumb and forefinger as you walk and let it swing freely and naturally. This not only helps you get rid of tension, but conveys a nice feeling for the rhythm of the golf swing itself.

If you feel anger after playing a particularly horrendous shot, try British teaching pro Ken Adwick's trick. Keep your fingers fully outstretched for a while. It's hard to stay mad when you can't make a fist.

If your opponent infuriates you with a lucky shot or some unwarranted gamesmanship, stall for time. Back off from your pre-shot routine until the distracting element is out of your mind.

Walking a course gives you many more chances to stretch or bend and thus stay relaxed than does playing polo-style from a golf cart. Many times you are required to take a cart, especially on resort courses, but you don't have to ride in it. If the golfer you're sharing the cart with is offended at your walking, tell him it's doctor's orders. If he's smart, he'll at least take turns walking and riding on alternate holes with you.

If you're unexpectedly held up at some point in your round, take a couple of extra practice swings rather than standing there club in hand, or engage a playing companion in light conversation so that you don't dwell on the wrong things.

Breathing deeply a few times is one of the best ways to reduce tension or nervousness prior to making a particularly important putt, especially if you have to wait for two or three other players to putt before you. It's a part of every good relaxation technique and produces consistent results.

The relaxed mind can also visualize better. Skiers preparing for the Olympics a few years ago used exercises before training which involved alternately tensing and relaxing all the muscle groups in the body. This is one of numerous relatively simple methods of proven effectiveness for slowing down the heartbeat and breathing and producing a feeling of inner calm. The skiers found that these exercises improved their ability to practice mentally and ultimately to perform.

Meditation techniques can achieve similar results. So can TM, mind control, biofeedback training, autogenics, yoga, or a trip to your local hypnotist.

Some of these techniques require a carefully cultivated attitude of indifference toward results or performance. The focus is on the act, not the outcome. Importing them into golf may require some modification to be effective. For example, chanting a mantra in the privacy of your home may work fine, but it would be disconcerting on the golf course.

We'll be seeing many more efforts to use mind-influencing systems in sport in the future. For the present, we think the logical way for most golfers to relax is within golf's natural framework—using the time and space around you to create a pleasant worry-free mood and a calm, methodical approach for every shot.

While over-arousal is a more common problem among club golfers, many veteran touring pros have the problem of too little arousal. Sometimes they have to make themselves "get up" for their week-in, week-out tournament schedule.

This does not mean they're immune to tension if they happen to be among the front runners on Sunday, just because they were under-aroused when they got into town on Tuesday. As Frank Beard notes, "Everybody backs up on the final day, and the guy who backs up the slowest is the winner."

Arousal is also relative to the occasion. "I don't get nervous at the Masters or Open anymore," Hale Irwin once said, "but I do get more interested."

At the club level, golfers may play a sociable member-guest without a trace of nervousness, but they also get "more interested" whenever they're playing for the club championship or the local city title.

If you are under-aroused, you can set some special goals for yourself for the day, such as hitting more fairways than usual. An interesting bet will also usually eliminate the blahs.

If you feel physically lethargic, run in place or do calisthenics to get your blood moving. But don't go overboard. For golf, it's better for most people to feel on the weak side than on the strong side. In this respect, weak connotes loose and long, strong connotes short and tight. That way you're less likely to start overswinging. This explains why golfers playing with the flu or some other complaint often will have good rounds. Physically, they're not feeling the muscular tension they normally would. And psychologically they have a built-in excuse for poor play, so there is no pressure to prove themselves. They attempt to do less and they often do more.

"I just fell asleep out there" is a phrase club golfers and tour players alike use to describe certain indifferent rounds that are the result of under-arousal. One way to prevent an excess of such indifferent play is to occasionally remind yourself that it really doesn't take much more time or effort to try to do it right than it does to perform indifferently. This attitude of giving every shot its best possible chance to succeed is certain to result in better shotmaking and in greater personal satisfaction.

26 THE EMOTIONAL EMERGENCY ROOM

Golfer A:

"I was really up for a certain one-day tournament at the club. I got there early, hit a bucket of balls, practiced putting, and my partner and I reached our assigned hole—it was a shotgun start—in plenty of time. Our opponents came late, and I spent 10 minutes pacing the tee. When they finally showed up, I was so mad I topped my tee shot 20 yards into the rough."

Golfer B:

"I was even with my opponent until the 17th, where I hit an approach to within seven feet of the cup. Immediately, I figured I had the guy. I thought I'd win that hole and play out the 18th carefully to win 1 up. Then he hit his approach inside mine. This tore me up completely. I missed my putt, played sloppy on 18 and lost 2 up."

Something more deeply felt than over-arousal is reported in these situations.

Golfer A wasn't just annoyed, he was livid.

Golfer B wasn't just disappointed, he was devastated.

It's easy enough to interpret what happened in terms of the two-hemisphere brain in each instance and to show how the destructive effects of the emotions on the golfers' games might have been prevented.

The first golfer might have coped with the unexpected delay by practicing short chips near the tee, say, or getting involved in a conversation with his partner about something unrelated to the match.

The second golfer might have followed our earlier advice against counting your birdies before they hatch and so have been much less vulnerable when he saw his opponent's good shot.

We can safely say what situations will tend to create tension and nervousness in the golfer, and so, as we did in the previous chapter, make some recommendations for helping golfers in those situations.

But we can't really predict in advance where and when the deep emotions will grip the golfer — where arousal will turn into outright fear or anger, for instance. The game and the golfer both have too many unexpected possibilities for us to confidently list situations that would be "emotion-prone" for most of us.

If you're running away from a tornado or a tidal wave, the extra adrenalin in your system produced by fear may spur you into doing the four-minute mile you need to save your life.

If you're in a hockey game or football game and get mad because you were high-sticked or missed a block, your anger may make you play more aggressively and so probably will help your team more.

But in golf, fear and anger are seldom, if ever, helpful. They cloud the mind and introduce tension in the body, thereby spoiling swing rhythm. They trip up both ANALYZER and INTEGRATOR.

In addition to having destructive physiological symptoms when you get mad or fearful, you also acquire the problem of *noticing* these symptoms. Once you're aware of rapid heartbeat, sweaty palms, irregular breathing, a cottony feeling in your mouth and an unstable condition in your lower legs, it's hard to think and play well.

Golf's three major sources of frustration

Earlier in this book we mentioned three aspects of golf that make it particularly frustrating to *learn*. There are three things about the game that make it particularly frustrating to *play* at times, too. If you're not aware of them, they'll take you by surprise and provoke unexpectedly deep emotional responses that will surely upset your play.

1. The game's small margin for error.

A film crew came to Augusta one year to do a short movie on the teacher-pupil relationship of Jack Grout and Jack Nicklaus.

After shooting the two men in various poses on the practice range for an hour, the director brought them over to a nearby tee to get the last of the footage he needed. There, his instructions to Nicklaus were to hit a drive, then walk down the hole side by side with Grout. With the long shadows of late afternoon falling across the fairway, it would make a dramatic closing scene for the movie.

Nicklaus listened, nodded, teed up his ball, then just before the cameras began to turn, he gave the director a look and said, "I suppose you want me to hit it down the middle?"

It had not crossed the filmmaker's mind that the great Jack Nicklaus could possibly hit a golf ball anywhere but dead center in the fairway. But it had crossed Jack's.

And that's really the point—even in those airy reaches where the Joneses, Hagens, Hogans, Players, Palmers and Nicklauses play, golf is too capricious a game ever to take for granted.

The body has to function with the precision of a slide rule during the golf swing in order to get consistent results. Slight deviations in grip pressure or swing plane or weight transfer usually produce catastrophic changes in the flight of the ball.

Assuming a 250-yard drive, if the face of your driver is three degrees open at impact, for instance, your tee shot will finish some 30 yards wide of the target. If you putt ¼ inch off center toward the toe or heel, you'll miss an otherwise straight 10-foot putt on a good quality green by one inch, a 20-foot putt by about six inches, and a 30-foot putt by at least 12 inches.

All we're saying is, if you realize the extraordinary amount of precision and skill involved, you won't be as likely to get angry when you do mis-hit a drive or miss a putt. And you won't be as fearful of failure every time you face a tight shot or tough putt—because you'll know a certain amount of failure is normal and inevitable.

2. The game's apparent unfairness.

Golf was not designed with fairness in mind, in the usual sense of the word "fairness," but we are a "fair-play" minded people—so we occasionally become incensed by what happens to our shots during a round.

A great tee shot winds up in a terrible lie.

A gust of wind takes a well-stroked approach wide of the green.

A tap-in misses the cup because of a worm cast.

These apparent injustices provoke strong emotions in golfers who are not aware of the fact that bad luck is part of the game.

Golfers who do realize the game was meant to be played outdoors on uneven terrain, and not on Astroturf, find it much easier to live with unexpected bad lies and will not be as likely to escalate one misfortune into an 8 on the hole, or a long string of double bogeys.

3. The game's uncompromisingly objective and lingering feedback.

There's no way to gloss over a bad performance in golf as you so often can in almost any other activity. Every shot is there to be measured in yards, feet and inches and in relation to where it was supposed to have landed.

A bad performance in a team sport can be obscured or rationalized, but in golf you are solely responsible for each shot you hit and for the score you turn in at the end of the day.

Even in a competitive, one-on-one sport such as tennis, where individual performance is seemingly highly visible, it is relatively easy to forget about bad shots as play continues and to project most losses onto factors outside your control, such as your opponent having a great backhand or serve.

In golf, you and your shot stand naked before the world—and you do so for minutes on end. If you're not careful a bad shot will stay with you, psychologically, for much longer than the time it takes to hit the next shot. Some bad shots never seem to go away—golfers will come up to a hole they haven't played in 15 years and suddenly vividly recall a duck-hook they produced there the last time they played.

And once you start playing a round of golf, the only thing that can happen to your score is that it will increase. Once you've lost a stroke, it's gone.

In fact, if you make a bad shot then put pressure on your swing to make a great recovery, chances are good you'll produce another bad shot. Harry Vardon best described it when he said, "Trying to do in three what should normally require four often ends up taking five."

What we're really saying is that there are times when golf requires not psychology so much as the philosophy "to get on with it."

Bobby Locke, in whom the emotions were contained as harmoniously as in anyone, had a playing temperament that was once described as "benign imperturbability." This mood consisted of staying relaxed, playing one shot at a time, and allowing for the fact that the outcome of at least one out of every five shots you play would be affected by luck as much as skill.

Golfers who don't fully appreciate the game's inherent difficulties are the ones most readily perturbed and most often victimized by fear or anger, or both.

Joy and despair

While we're on the subject of philosophy, two other strong feelings—joy and despair—ought to be briefly mentioned, as they, too, can put you in the emotional emergency room.

Unbridled joy can be as bad for your game as

fear or anger because it triggers similar reactions. If you perform a victory dance after sinking a 50-foot putt and it disrupts your tee-shot routine on the next hole, causing you to drive O.B., it's just as harmful as if you missed a gimme putt because you choked or got mad.

When playing well, but in control of his emotions, Tom Watson once described the feeling as "an inner calm." Al Geiberger called it "controlled enthusiasm."

"It was a very strange kind of first two months that I played," Bruce Lietzke once recalled of a winning spell he enjoyed. "I played confidently and almost subconsciously, but I played with very little emotion—like a machine or robot."

In other words, the most functional mood for golf is without lows or highs. This seems like just another example of golf's unfairness—you go out on the course for enjoyment, but if you are playing for all the marbles, you are not allowed to enjoy triumph until you get off the course.

The fact is, you can enjoy a string of birdies or pars. But the idea is to experience your run of good luck objectively, with restraint. Don't get carried away.

Despair is quitting—on the hole, on the round, on yourself. There's a practical reason for not quitting in golf. The game is unpredictable. You never really know what's going to happen next.

All great players know there are days when no matter what they do, the game wins. Nicklaus said after shooting in the 80's at Pebble Beach one year, "Well, it finally caught up with me." When Walter Hagen finished 53rd in his first British Open, he was asked why he had kept trying so hard on the last day and he shrugged, "Because 53rd is better than 54th."

But for every story of obvious and continuing disaster on the golf course, one can also be cited to show how a hopeless cause became a victory. Jerry Barber once made putts from 20 feet, 40 feet and 60 feet on the last three holes to come from behind to win the 1961 PGA Championship, by tying with Don January and winning the playoff.

Billy Casper was down seven shots to Lee Trevino with five holes to go in the Alcan Championship in 1969, yet wound up winning. He was down to Arnold Palmer seven shots with nine holes to play in the 1966 Open at Olympic Club, but hung in and won.

The point is you never know what's going to happen in golf if you resist despair and keep trying. But you'll never experience the unexpected if you quit.

PART V
FINDING YOUR OWN STYLE

27 FINDING YOUR OWN PLAYING STYLE

A basic weapon of the golf hustler is advice: "Does your left heel always come up like that?"

It would be nice if we could nonchalantly counter with: "Yeah, just like Nicklaus'."

But most of us can't do that convincingly. Instead, we tend to dwell on the technicality and it hurts our swing. The hustler's goal is achieved—we swing with our mind still locked firmly in the ANALYZER setting.

U. of Alabama golf coach Conrad Rehling notes, "Golf is one of the few games where there are more teachers than players," and fellow golfers unwittingly wreak as much havoc as the hustlers with their unsolicited gems of instructional wisdom.

If a friend says, "Try standing closer to the ball," and the comment promotes an excessively detailed awareness of swing technique, it prevents us from switching control to our INTEGRATOR and making our very best swing.

We said earlier that too much *feeling* turns INTEGRATOR into DISINTEGRATOR.

Well, too much *detail* turns ANALYZER into PARALYZER.

The single most effective and lasting protection against this happening is a solid, logical working knowledge of your own playing style.

The golf swing may be simple in theory but the machine which performs it is very complicated. If you don't know how or why your particular "machine" works most effectively in golf, then you will be more susceptible to doubt and indecision when you are playing, and more likely to listen to rash or meaningless advice. The better you know your swing, the less you'll have to think about it.

How does one understand the golf swing?

First, recognize that there is no one swing for all players. A great many techniques and combinations of techniques can work. This has been shown in practice through the immense number of vastly different swing stylists who have succeeded on the tour.

This fact has also been demonstrated theoretically in a book which came out a few years ago, called *The Search for the Perfect Swing*. Physicist-author Alastair Cochran and golf writer John Stobbs put it together after several years of research with specialists in anatomy, ballistics, biomechanics, engineering, medicine, physical education and physiology.

This book—the ultimate statement by the analytical left hemisphere on how the golf swing works—concluded that, although a model can be constructed exemplifying sound principles, there is in fact no perfect golf swing. Rather, there are a variety of possibilities that are functional and can be considered correct as long as they do not violate physical law.

This is where the critical judgment of your own ANALYZER (or your golf professional's) becomes a major factor. You must evaluate your assets and liabilities to determine the individual *preferences* that work best to bring about the sound *principles* to influence the inviolable *laws*.

For example, ball-flight laws reflect the physical forces of nature and they must work every time, without fail. At the moment of impact, the ball is not affected by swing style, but rather by purely functional things such as clubhead speed, the path on which the clubhead is traveling, the clubface position, angle of descent and squareness of contact.

Speed, then, is a law; the velocity with which the clubhead is traveling directly influences the distance the ball will go.

Principles are at the next level of importance. They are factors of high order which have direct relation to and influence on the laws, but reflect a certain amount of subjective judgment about mechanics of the swing.

The two-lever system is a sound principle for generating clubhead speed, for example. When you transfer from a one-lever system (which would occur if you swung the club with no wrist cock) to a two-lever system consisting of the left arm and club and created as the wrist is cocked, you multiply the potential force considerably.

Preferences constitute a third and final level of priorities in establishing a golf swing, yet in a sense they are the most important because it is at this level that we most often work. A preference is the act of choosing or liking better some particular approach, method, device, etc., over all others.

For example, if you need more than one lever in the arm-and-club relationship (and you do if you desire distance), the question is where should you create this second lever—or where to cock your wrist? Early? In mid-swing? At the top of the swing? On the downswing? Or even before you start the backswing?

A strong, young high-schooler might be able to cock his wrists early, be all over the place on his backswing and gain clubhead speed without sacrificing control. An old-timer would lose more of his already diminishing arc width if he "set" the wrist cock early, so he would probably be better off taking it back Walter Hagen-style, even if it added a bit of a sway.

Knowledge of how your swing works best may be gained exclusively through trial and error. But one flaw in a totally intuitive approach to mastering the game is that when your swing does go off track—and it surely will—it may be harder for you to locate the problem. This is when it's important to have the objective viewpoint of a professional teacher.

Some avid engineer/golfers in Tampa are working on a system for tracking the golf swing electronically and, with the aid of a computer, tracing a "picture" of the swing that would show the swing plane, clubhead acceleration and clubface alignment throughout the swing. The idea being, if you get a picture of your golf swing when it's working well, then one day when it goes off track you can go and get another tracing. By superimposing it on the first one, you will be able to see at a glance what you're doing differently.

Until such technology comes of age, golfers with an awareness of the laws, principles and preferences affecting their golf swing have an edge over the total "by-feel" players in determining faults and making sensible corrections.

Finding your swing may involve a process not unlike that the typical adolescent goes through in establishing his or her identity. The youngster experiments with different roles, voices, opinions and relationships until he finally comes up with the personality most closely reflecting what he is.

The golfer seeking maturity in his game may have to do the same thing in sorting out all the swing variables, before he arrives at the method that works best for him on the golf course. Like the adolescent, the searching golfer may at first be preoccupied with appearance—how the swing looks—but when he wises up, the only thing that matters is substance—how the swing functions to produce low scores.

This pragmatic approach is summed up in a phrase heard on tour:

"If your swing works, don't fix it."

28 FINDING YOUR OWN PSYCHOLOGICAL STYLE

If you study the swing techniques of the great players of the past half-century, you'll be amazed at how many different styles have developed for achieving the game's main objective, of moving a ball from here to there in the least number of strokes.

Although these styles vary in appearance they have effectively dealt with ball-flight laws and observed the principles of swing mechanics required to produce winning rounds of golf. But perhaps the main reason for the diversity lies in the vast array of individual preferences reflected. The great players developed swings that not only conform to laws and principles of golf—but conform to their own individual physical make-ups. They developed games which were, in effect, custom-made for their bodily preferences.

The argument for recognizing the importance of individual differences in physical-mechanical styles is fairly apparent.

But it's just as important to recognize individual differences in psychological technique, too. What works wonders for Lee Trevino in managing his thoughts between shots on the course may prove disastrous to a golfer with different mental and emotional needs. Artificially changing your style for the game may not work even if in theory it is in your best interests as a golfer. If you're naturally spontaneous and impulsive, but force yourself to deliberate carefully about every shot you play (because you've seen Nicklaus do it that way), the change in style won't feel right. What you may gain in better planning from your lengthier pre-shot routines, you may lose because of increased tension.

In other words, the style for winning the mind game in golf must also be custom-made to a large extent, so that it accurately reflects your individual psychological make-up.

Psychological "laws" are not as precise as physical laws, but in this book we distinguish three aspects of the mind that are sufficiently real to use as a base for building your own guiding principles and personal preferences for your mental game.

They are 1) the two-hemisphere brain, 2) the personality, and 3) the emotions. It would be useful to summarize what we have said about these three factors now, and to note the potential for individual variation within each one.

Fact: you have a two-hemisphere brain

During a round of golf, the ANALYZER side of your brain helps you primarily in preparing for each shot. It helps you evaluate the lie of the ball, the course and weather conditions, and the type of shot you are planning. It helps you to select the proper club and to devise intelligent shotmaking tactics for each hole.

The INTEGRATOR side of your brain plays some role in the pre-shot routine—it helps you visualize the shot you're planning to make, for example—but its main job is to "get it all together" for you at the time of execution. Its special intuitive, body-in-space powers help you make the transition from the pre-swing preparation to the in-swing mechanics each time a shot is played.

Some golfers play the game almost exclusively with one hemisphere or the other, which is the mental equivalent of playing with half a set of clubs.

Other golfers frequently go to one hemisphere for something that only the other hemisphere can supply and thereby spoil shots. They analyze when they should be integrating and integrate when they should be analyzing. Still other golfers mis-hit shots because ANALYZER and INTEGRATOR are interfering with each other or not communicating at all.

An effective and also enjoyable way to discover individual differences in your own ANALYZER/ INTEGRATOR functioning is to construct a psychological scorecard for your round from time to time. This diagnostic tool 1) creates an awareness of general traits in your psychological make-up which alone may be sufficient to help you to improve and 2) gives you information about specific shot execution. This can help you process bad shots in the future without getting upset about them or causing you to alter your swing mechanics unnecessarily.

The crucial moment in the ANALYZER/INTEGRATOR partnership occurs just prior to making the swing. The most effective method for building the bridge from thought to action—for putting your ANALYZER on stand-by and letting your INTEGRATOR do its thing—is to use a swing cue. This is a favorite evocative word or phrase, an image, or even a drill or exercise that elicits the good swing consistently.

The best time to establish swing cues of any kind is when you're playing well. The more accurately you pin down the feeling of the swing at that time, the easier it will be to retrieve it at a later date and repeat the same good performance. Your own psychological make-up dictates the type of swing cue you use. Some golfers can use verbal, visual or kinesthetic swing cues interchangeably with equal effectiveness in bridging the gap from ANALYZER to INTEGRATOR. Others do markedly better using only one type of cue. And if they use verbal cues, they may prefer kine cues to chunker cues or vice versa. If they are strong visualizers, they may prefer "seeing" shots in motion-picture form—as Nicklaus and Johnny Miller do. For other golfers, that technique may produce just a blur—these people may image their swing quite effectively in something like snapshot form.

Distractions—from within and without—can affect the golfer's ability to make proper use of the two-hemisphere brain out on the golf course. There are various diversionary tactics which can be employed between shots to keep your ANALYZER occupied—so it does not engender overly technical considerations about the game—and to prevent your INTEGRATOR's emotional tendencies from getting out of hand. Your own psychological make-up will determine which tactics work best for you.

For the time required to actually plan and make each shot, distractions must be totally blocked out to make a clear, sensible decision about the shot at hand and to execute smoothly. Call a 30-second social moratorium before every shot for this purpose. If you can concentrate this long for every shot, you'll be able to draw on your ANALYZER to do all the pre-shot analysis necessary, and to transfer control to your INTEGRATOR, which has the image and feeling of your good swing when the moment comes to start the club back.

Thirty seconds is a guideline. You may need more time or less to perform at your best in the average shot situation you face. It depends on your personal psychological preference.

The state of the body can influence the mood of the mind. In golf, this somatopsychic effect can remove tension in three ways at the physical level, which in turn tends to dissipate tension felt at the mental level:

1. through a pre-round routine of warm-up drills, which helps the body make the transition from off-course activities to actual play more smoothly;

2. through a fixed pre-shot routine, which keeps the body in a more relaxed state before every shot;

3. through a rehearsal-swing routine, which helps the body stay relaxed on short shots and trouble shots that are intrinsically more anxiety-producing.

All three routines pave the way for the best possible ANALYZER/INTEGRATOR partnership in the individual. But exactly *how* you warm up for a round of golf, *how* you organize your pre-shot tasks and *how* you prepare for executing trouble shots is a matter of individual style. Jim Simons needs 12 seconds to set up and hit a fairway wedge.

Lanny Wadkins does it in only three seconds. It depends on what makes a player feel most comfortable, psychologically, and what produces the best results during actual play.

There are many methods of physical and mental practice, of varying effectiveness, which depend on the psychological make-up of the individual golfer.

Progress in golf, as in most endeavors, is usually made more readily when the individual has an accurate and up-to-date understanding of his status in the game, and a set of realistic goals to sustain interest and motivation. A golfer's journal is a tool that players can use to keep track of their progress in practice and in play. It can be used to store swing cues, write down goals, and record scores, tactical information on different holes and courses, and notes on mechanics and techniques. It need not be this extensive—or it can be *more* extensive. The format of a golfer's journal, and the zeal and regularity with which it is kept, is once again a matter of individual preference.

Fact: you have a personality

In golf, the personality serves as a kind of giant umbrella, influencing and affecting the ANALYZER/INTEGRATOR mind work we have described. But since every person is unique, the exact manner in which the personality can and should affect the two-hemisphere game necessarily varies from golfer to golfer.

There are four key aspects of personality as they relate to golf and to the effort we are making here to show the range of psychological differences.

They are: 1) self-concept; 2) style of responding to immediate events; 3) attitude of control (or non-control) toward the things around us; and 4) the overall maturity of our personality in relation to our performance.

1). The single most important aspect of personality within our means to change is the ongoing image we create of ourselves as golfers—how we see ourselves, and how highly we value what we see.

Some players have a naturally positive self-concept that is just right for promoting their progress in golf. Others may be overly confident, still others unnecessarily hard on themselves. Since a realistically positive self-concept fosters better achievement, it is in the interest of every golfer to develop such a portrait. How you talk to yourself, in whatever mode is natural for you on the golf course, reflects that portrait. The extent to which you can slant your internal dialogue favorably and optimistically will determine how positive your self-concept will become and the better will be your chances of playing your best possible shots.

2). The way we respond mentally to the good or bad shots we hit can affect the rest of our game. A debriefing session after every shot provides an opportunity to mentally reinforce favorable swing results and to neutralize the unfavorable ones. It also is a process that leaves the golfer psychologically fresh for the next shot. But exactly how the debriefing should be conducted is up to the individual.

3). The degree of personal control we feel we exert over golf is an aspect of personality that affects our play. The question as to whether a person is in charge of his environment, or in the hands of it, becomes a problem in golf if one has an exaggerated notion either way.

Are you more naturally a "make-it-happen" personality, or a "let-it-happen" personality? Within that range there is a choice of places where you belong, and the place you occupy should be where you're most comfortable.

4). The degree of maturity of our personality dictates whether or not golf will trap us into thinking and acting like adolescents. The three most common types of egocentric or self-conscious behavior that can cost golfers strokes are:

—thinking about what other golfers are thinking of you as you prepare to hit;

—inventing stories about what happens to you on the course as a way of avoiding confronting certain limitations or weaknesses in your game;

—making false assumptions about your abilities, such as thinking you can hit your 5-iron 180 yards every time you use it on the course, just because you reached that distance with it one time at the range.

Fact: you have emotions

The mind's power source—the last element in our model of the new golf mind—is that pool of fundamental life energies and emotions that creates distinctive human personalities and drives people to try to excel in things like golf in the first place.

The two most important emotional variables related to on-course performance that are created and partly controlled by the individual golfer's own psychological make-up are arousal and coping with pressure.

The amount of arousal needed for golf is a personal variable to a degree. We all need to experience some emotional arousal to play golf well. But an under-aroused golfer has little or no activity in either hemisphere and consequently no traffic moving on the bridge between his hemispheres. On the other hand, an over-aroused golfer has a traffic jam on the bridge between hemispheres. Too much excitement or tension inhibits and confuses the left-right partnership.

Each golfer has an optimal range or level of arousal that is right for him. For example, if you need to get to the golf course two hours before tee-off time to get cranked up physically and psychologically for a big match, then that's what it takes to reach your personal arousal level. If you're a more excitable type and prefer to get to the course with just a few minutes to spare to keep from getting over-stimulated, then that's what you should do.

How golfers cope with pressure is the other major emotional variable. For example, 50 years apart, Bobby Jones and Tom Watson each read books on the eve of winning major championships.

Jones read Pappini's *Life of Christ* and Watson studied a CAB aircraft manual. But the function of the reading was identical—to keep the mind preoccupied so thoughts about the next day's competition wouldn't intervene and create worries or deplete energies. In between the eras of these stars, Walter Hagen found another way to do it which, of course, was to socialize. During one drinking session prior to a big match with Leo Diegel, one of Hagen's friends reported with some concern:

"Walter, Leo's in bed."

"Yeah," said Hagen, lifting his glass, "but he ain't sleeping."

Effectively coping with pressure on the course is another area where individual choice must be exercised. Does talking to your playing partners help you stay relaxed? Does recalling a past successful shot do the trick? How about focusing on some pleasant attribute of the natural setting? Or does it take something physical—a few deep-knee bends, say—to prevent the choke? These and many other methods are all perfectly valid and functional—if they suit you.

Finding your own effective psychological style is really the ultimate achievement of the new golf mind. It is the result of total self-awareness as a golfer. It means you have come to understand and to accept yourself as a person to such an extent that on the golf course you are able to use your own unique mental, emotional and psychological equipment to your benefit. It means you've won the mind game.